IPSWICH TOWN
Champions of England
1961-1962

Ipswich Town: Champions of England 1961-62   1-874287-56-2
Ipswich Town: The Modern Era – A Complete Record   1-874287-43-0
Bristol City: The Modern Era – A Complete Record   1-874287-28-7
Cambridge United: The League Era – A Complete Record   1-874287-32-5
Cambridge United: 101 Golden Greats   1-874287-58-9
Colchester United: Graham to Whitton – A Complete Record   1-874287-27-9
Coventry City: The Elite Era – A Complete Record   1-874287-51-1
Coventry City: An Illustrated History   1-874287-36-8
History of the Everton Football Club 1878-1928   1-874287-14-7
Halifax Town: From Ball to Lillis – A Complete Record   1-874287-26-0
Hereford United: The League Era – A Complete Record   1-874287-18-X
Luton Town: The Modern Era – A Complete Record   1-874287-05-8
Luton Town: An Illustrated History   1-874287-37-6
Peterborough United: The Modern Era – A Complete Record   1-874287-33-3
Peterborough United: Who's Who   1-874287-48-1
Plymouth Argyle: The Modern Era – A Complete Record   1-874287-54-6
Plymouth Argyle: 101 Golden Greats   1-874287-47-3
Portsmouth: From Tindall to Ball – A Complete Record   1-874287-25-2
Portsmouth: Champions of England – 1948-49 & 1949-50   1-874287-38-4
The Romance of the Wednesday 1867-1926   1-874287-17-1
Stoke City: 101 Golden Greats   1-874287-46-5
Stoke City: The Modern Era – A Complete Record   1-874287-39-2
West Ham: From Greenwood to Redknapp   1-874287-19-8
West Ham: The Elite Era – A Complete Record   1-874287-31-7
Wimbledon: From Southern League to Premiership   1-874287-09-0
Wimbledon: From Wembley to Selhurst   1-874287-20-1
Wimbledon: The Premiership Years   1-874287-40-6
Wrexham: The Modern Era – A Complete Record   1-874287-52-X
Aberdeen: A Centenary History 1903-2003   1-874287-49-X
Aberdeen: The European Era – A Complete Record   1-874287-11-2
The Story of the Celtic 1888-1938   1-874287-15-5
The Story of the Rangers 1873-1923   1-874287-16-3
Red Dragons in Europe – A Complete Record   1-874287-01-5
The Book of Football: A History to 1905-06   1-874287-13-9
England's Quest for the World Cup – A Complete Record   1-874287-61-9
Scotland: The Quest for the World Cup – A Complete Record   1-897850-50-6
Ireland: The Quest for the World Cup – A Complete Record   1-897850-80-8

IPSWICH TOWN
CHAMPIONS OF ENGLAND
1961-62

Series Editor: Clive Leatherdale

Rob Hadgraft

Desert Island Books

First Published in 2002

DESERT ISLAND BOOKS LIMITED
89 Park Street, Westcliff-on-Sea, Essex SS0 7PD
United Kingdom
www.desertislandbooks.com

© 2002 Rob Hadgraft

The right of Rob Hadgraft to be identified as author of this work has been asserted
under The Copyright Designs and Patents Act 1988

British Library Cataloguing-in-Publication Data
A catalogue record for this book is available from the British Library

ISBN 1-874287-56-2 (Cloth case)
ISBN 1-874287-63-5 (paperback)

Printed in Great Britain
by
The Cromwell Press, Trowbridge, Wilts

Photographs in this book are reproduced by kind permission
of the Dave Kindred collection

~ *Contents* ~

~ *Foreword* ~

by John Motson OBE

The 1961-62 football season was significant for me for two distinct reasons. At Christmas 1961, I left Culford School, Bury St Edmunds, to pursue a career in journalism which eventually led to my present position as a BBC football commentator.

However, in my last term at school, I had the pleasure of watching Alf Ramsey's Ipswich Town, who had just been promoted as Second Division champions, storm fearlessly through their First Division programme on their way to winning the title at the first attempt.

What an Autumn that was! Burnley, one of the early visitors to Portman Road, were beaten 6-2; Ipswich put four past Birmingham City and West Ham United; then my father and I saw Manchester United – Bobby Charlton and all – put to the sword with two goals from Ted Phillips and one each from John Elsworthy and Ray Crawford.

In those days my dad and I nursed a little affection for Chelsea, but come December they took a 5-2 beating at Portman Road with a rampant Crawford scoring a hat-trick.

Come the second half of the season, when I was living back in London, I saw three games in the capital which virtually assured Ipswich of the championship. A 3-1 victory at White Hart Lane over the title-holders Tottenham, a 2-2 draw in the return at Stamford Bridge, and then a memorable 3-0 win at Arsenal on Easter Monday.

It was one of the great fairy tales of post-war football, and laid the foundation for 40 years of happy familiarity between Ipswich Town and myself.

What a pleasure it was for me to meet so many members of that 1962 team at the reunion dinner held at Portman Road at the end of the 2001-02 season. They will never be forgotten!

John Motson
July 2002

~ *Author's Note* ~

One of my earliest football memories is having a perfect view of Ipswich's Ray Crawford diving gracefully to head a picture goal at Portman Road in the 1960s. It was a Second Division game and Crawford was the returning hero, enjoying his second spell at the club. As a wide-eyed schoolboy, I didn't understand why the home fans called him 'Jungle Boy', but from his performance and demeanour on the pitch I could see exactly why he was so popular.

A few years earlier the same player had spearheaded a triumphant 1961-62 campaign at Ipswich that was so unexpected it would have stretched even the tolerance of *Roy of the Rovers'* readers! Crawford's 33 goals had, unbelievably, helped his humble club become Champions of England at the first attempt. This book commemorates the 40th anniversary of those events, yet the scale of the achievement has still not sunk in for some of those who witnessed it.

I was pleased to have the opportunity, via this book, to examine in detail the fascinating events that led up to, and occurred after, Town skipper Andy Nelson lifted the championship trophy. As ever, the people at Ipswich Town FC were welcoming and co-operative and I am indebted to many individuals from Suffolk and further afield who recounted their memories or assisted in some way with research.

In no particular order, I would like to thank Pat Godbold, John Elsworthy, John Eastwood, Jim Crane, Steve Prentice, Andy Nelson, John Bloom, Elvin King, Mick Banthorpe, Elizabeth Montgomery, Tim Quelch, Alasdair Ross, Paul Browes, Paul Jarman, Mark Jarman, David Hird, Roger Wash, Jim French, Ralph Morris, Nick Garnham, Ian Sale, David Sheepshanks and the late John Finch. Sadly, local legend Ron Ellis died before this project got under way and I was unable to tap into his remarkable memory and enthusiasm. Many thanks to the BBC's ever-popular John Motson for interrupting his busy schedule to provide the foreword, Dave Kindred for the pictorial content, and my wife Katie for support and encouragement.

Rob Hadgraft
September 2002

~ *The Most Unlikely Champions* ~

On Saturday, 28 April 1962, shortly after 4.20pm, Ipswich Town's Scottish half-back Billy Baxter was impeded by an Aston Villa forward as he attempted to launch another desperate attack on the Churchman's End at a packed Portman Road. The whistle sounded for a free-kick. Little winger Roy Stephenson bustled over and placed the ball close to the touchline. He took several steps back and glanced up towards the crowded penalty area to size up where to aim his kick. The whole ground expected a long, high cross towards the penalty spot – and that's exactly what he produced. Up soared 6ft-plus Welsh half-back John Elsworthy to meet the swinging ball firmly with his head. He judged its flight perfectly. The ball glided goalwards and an expectant crowd held its breath. With goalkeeper Nigel Sims floundering, lanky right-back Gordon Lee leaped vertically to try to block the ball on the goalline. It thumped against the crossbar above him and rebounded out, leaving Lee tumbling backwards into the net and Sims marooned out of position. Quick as a flash, Ipswich's ace marksman Ray Crawford flung himself forward from the six-yard line and headed the rebound firmly into the net.

The roar from the 28,932 crowd was deafening. After 72 minutes of stalemate, during which Town had rarely looked like scoring, the explosion of noise was fuelled by relief and pent-up tension as much as joy. Pre-match optimism had been slowly eroded by Villa's unexpected resilience, but now the Town fans were once again convinced their humble team was about to make football history. Incredibly, the Football League championship was within Ipswich's grasp.

All it needed was for Town to cling to their lead in this final game, and for off-form Burnley to slip up. The Lancashire club had to win their remaining two games to prevent Town taking the title – but that wouldn't be easy for them to do. Harry Potts' skilful and experienced side were struggling in the face of a congested fixture list as they chased a League and FA Cup double. They'd won only one of their previous eight League matches and were exhausted and injury-hit after playing six games in the preceding fourteen days.

In mid-February, Burnley had been four points clear at the top with games in hand, but over subsequent weeks their collapse was startling. Losing key forward Jimmy McIlroy for several games with a thigh injury was certainly a serious blow, but tiredness and dwindling confidence also played a big part in allowing Town to remain firmly in the race. Burnley players recall with disbelief how they let things slip in the League: Tommy Cummings called it a 'true tragedy', while McIlroy said 'we threw it away when we had it won'.

Town had notched up sensational late-season away wins at Spurs and Arsenal, and closed the gap in dramatic fashion. The popular view in the season's final week was that Ipswich would beat Villa, while Burnley, playing at home, would overcome already-relegated Chelsea. This would mean the title would then be decided two days later, when Burnley would have to win their final game, at Sheffield Wednesday. Before Town's last match, bookmakers Joe Coral offered odds of 4-5 on each of Town and Burnley lifting the trophy – and made Burnley hot favourites to beat Chelsea. The Football League apparently shared the bookies' view that the title would be decided on the Monday at Hillsborough, for there was no sign of the Championship trophy at Portman Road.

Before the game, Town had apparently promised to broadcast the latest score from Burnley at regular fifteen-minute intervals, but none of the supporters interviewed for this book recall that happening. Most relied on the large half-time scoreboards operated at the ground by the local paper, the *Evening Star*. These large wooden constructions involved white numbers, painted on black metal squares, being hung up on rows of nails alongside twenty letters of the alphabet. It could be decoded via the pocket-sized matchday programme, which showed that Burnley v Chelsea was match 'C'. Groans went up when the score-line 1-0 was revealed beside the 'C'. But midway through the second half, just minutes before Crawford's breakthrough goal, news somehow filtered through that it was now 1-1 at Turf Moor. That result would be enough for the title, provided Town now scored.

Up at a packed Turf Moor, Ian Towers had blasted the ball into the roof of an unguarded Chelsea net to put Burnley ahead, but the plucky Londoners had now equalised when Bobby Tambling's shot was deflected home by Frank Blunstone's backside. Supporter Ken Lewis remembers that news of Chelsea's equaliser was yelled from the

East Stand at Jimmy Leadbetter as the Town winger came across to take a corner. Leadbetter responded by clapping his hands in delight and shouting back that Town would score shortly to complete the job. How right he was.

Ipswich Town had only turned professional 25 years earlier and this was the club's very first season in the top flight. Although promoted as Division Two champions, few outside Suffolk expected anything other than a fight against relegation, now that Town were on the bigger stage. One bookmaker in Suffolk had even offered 500-1 back in August against Town winning the title. Ipswich were a team of cast-offs and ageing journeymen when compared to the likes of reigning double-winners Spurs or Matt Busby's rebuilt Manchester United. Quite apart from the humble, rural nature of their surroundings, Town were an elderly side largely bereft of well-known names. An exception was manager Alf Ramsey, a quiet and dignified former England full-back who shied away from publicity and went about his work with a minimum of fuss. The only widely-known player was goal-machine Crawford, although his strike partner Ted Phillips had also gained attention with his astonishing cannonball shooting. As the season had taken shape, the cynics grudgingly began to concede that this well-organised side were no mugs and were cleverly taking advantage of being an unknown quantity.

But could they take the title? Crawford's 72nd-minute break-through goal against Villa stung the Midlanders into action. With little to lose, they pushed nine men forward in search of an equaliser. This, of course, left them woefully short at the back, and when the ball was hooked high out of Town's box by Stephenson there was only blond defender John Sleeuwenhoek near the halfway line to prevent Crawford getting a clear run on goal. The Town man – adrenalin still pumping after his goal – somehow shook off his unpronounceable rival and sped off on a thrilling 40-yard run. Keeper Sims advanced out of goal and got a hand to the ball to knock it away, but Crawford was not to be denied. After briefly losing sight of the loose ball, he stretched acrobatically and hooked it viciously into the net. Two goals up with less than fifteen minutes remaining. Surely the points were safe now. *Wonderful Land* by The Shadows was topping the charts that week, and life was indeed exhilarating in this normally quiet corner of England. In the closing minutes jubilant Town had the ball in shell-shocked Sims' net twice more, but on both occasions they were ruled out for offside.

The only question that remained involved the scoreline 250 miles away at Turf Moor. Were Burnley still being held? In the pandemonium at Portman Road even those with radios couldn't be sure. In fact, Burnley's hopes were draining away in agonising fashion. As the final whistle drew closer, their score was still 1-1 and England international Ray Pointer had just missed a sitter, hitting a post when it had seemed easier to score.

The referee's whistle sounded at Portman Road and Town fans streamed onto the pitch. It remained unclear whether the title had been won, but nothing would stop this party. The players struggled towards the gap at the corner of the ground and the sanctuary of their ancient wooden dressing room, a former cricket pavilion positioned close to the Churchman's Stand. Thousands of fans milled around on the pitch and there was not a patch of green to be seen from the stands. Some players had made it off the pitch, but others were still out there when the Burnley news came through minutes later. It appears the first man in the ground to hear the details was Jim Gaughan, a reporter with the *London Evening News*. Amidst the mayhem of the pressbox, Gaughan pressed a phone to his ear and attempted to establish the Burnley score from a colleague at the other end of the line. The assembled throng watched spellbound as he slowly raised his arm and then jerked it upwards with an unmistakable thumbs-up gesture. A shout went up among the assembled hacks and rapidly spread through the stand, growing to a roar as it reached those out on the pitch. As this was happening, the club's tannoy man, Jack Hayward, in a broad Suffolk accent but in the formal manner of the times, stiffly announced: 'We have been informed that as a result of Burnley's 1-1 draw, Ipswich Town have won the Football League championship.'

A roar went up and the Town players already off the pitch reappeared, some of them stripped to the waist. Yet more fans squeezed onto the turf, where the focus of attention became the figures of Crawford and goalkeeper Roy Bailey, modest smiles on their faces as they were hoisted shoulder-high.

Champagne, some of it sent by TV football commentator Kenneth Wolstenholme, who lost a bet about Ipswich finishing higher than

Spurs, was cracked open and bottled beer was also distributed among the players. Long-serving trainer Jimmy Forsyth leaped fully clothed into the communal bath. For a few brief moments even the ice-cool Ramsey got carried away, and according to one reporter announced that he felt like 'jumping over the moon'. Was this how a football cliché was born? Barely half an hour after the final whistle, many telegrams and phone calls of congratulation had been taken in the club's modestly-appointed office. Reigning champions Tottenham and neighbours Colchester United were among the first to get their telegrams through and there was even one from Scotland, where former Town boss Scott Duncan was now based. The outspoken Burnley chairman Bob Lord swallowed his disappointment and managed to get through on the phone to say 'well done'.

When it came to the crunch, cultured Burnley and not naïve Ipswich had been the side to buckle under pressure and fatigue. Ramsey's loyal charges had raised their game when it mattered and the shell-shocked Clarets ended up falling short in both their League and Cup quests. Their League season ended with a 0-4 hammering at Hillsborough on the Monday, leaving Town title-winners by a clear three points. The good folk of East Lancashire generously acknowledged Town's triumph and Turf Moor devotee Tim Quelch recalls his personal agony only too well: 'Looking back, with all feelings of pain long gone, I have to recognise Ipswich's achievement. Typical of the players was Leadbetter, who looked more aged than TV copper Dixon of Dock Green. He was a ploddingly orthodox inside-left when he was with Chelsea and Brighton, but Ramsey transformed him.'

Quelch is right to single out Leadbetter as a key figure. Nicknamed 'Sticks' or 'Steptoe' because of his spindly frame, he looked far older than his 33 years, and many fans had been amazed he'd prospered in the Second Division, let alone in the top flight. He was perhaps the most unlikely among an entire team of unlikely heroes. Tottenham and Everton had also won successive Second and First Division championships (Ramsey played in the Spurs side), but both of those clubs had played in the top flight in the past, unlike greenhorns Ipswich. In addition, Town had become only the second club to win the championships of the First, Second and Third Divisions. Wolves were the other, but it took them 30 years to achieve the feat, while Ipswich completed the task in just six.

So how had they done it? Every successful underdog has an abundance of team spirit and Ipswich certainly had it in bucketloads. Ramsey and his men were a very close-knit bunch. A common sight after training would be the players' bicycles propped up outside Jim's Café in Princes Street, with their owners relaxing inside over a steaming mug of tea and plate of egg and chips.

The Suffolk public had responded in numbers to the new-found success. They flocked in from surrounding rural areas, the younger and shorter ones carrying little wooden stools or milk crates to stand on. Their representative at pitch level was the burly bus conductor 'Swede' Herring, a beaming eccentric from the Chantry housing estate, who wandered around before kick-off decked out in blue and white, bellowing at the locals to make more noise. Unaccustomed to the regular big crowds, many fans tended to cluster in the areas nearest the entrances to the terraces, which inevitably caused congestion. The real die-hards would arrive at the ground to queue up several hours before kick-off, but then get highly annoyed when latecomers were escorted around the pitch like VIPs to the less congested areas. Average attendances in 1961-62 shot up by around 50 percent and the stadium record was broken several times. Even the smallest gate of the season – just under 17,000 – was higher than the previous term's average.

Inevitably, the Ipswich success story was manna from heaven for the media. Celebrated writer Ian Wooldridge gushed about the 'most magnificent municipal hangover in history', after he found himself joining in celebrations after the Villa game, missing at least nine trains back to London in the process. Broadcaster David Coleman wrote: 'Soccer laughed good-naturedly at the thought of Ipswich in Division One. That was last year. Today Ipswich have earned the respect of every First Division club. They've proved their worth, not by flukes or the bludgeon, but by pure football played in a simple, direct way that leads to goals and movements of beauty.'

There was considerable civic pride too. The local council acknowledged that the football club had put the town on the map and, with the embarrassed Town manager looking on, Mayor of Ipswich Charlotte Green announced: 'Mr Ramsey is about the most unobtrusive man I know. But he must have a wonderful personality to have created such a team spirit. The pessimists who, at the beginning of this season were saying that the Town would be lucky to get off the bottom of the table, have all been confounded.'

Those pessimists could be forgiven. After all, the only money Ramsey spent on strengthening his Second Division championship squad was the £12,300 it took to bring inside-forward Doug Moran from Falkirk. It meant the team that subsequently won the League cost just £33,600. The widely-used 'country cousins' label was inaccurate in that only Phillips actually hailed from Suffolk, but 'journeymen and cast-offs' was certainly nearer the mark. The backbone of the team had been together for years, and five of them – Roy Bailey, Larry Carberry, Elsworthy, Phillips and Leadbetter – had already won championship medals in Division Three (South) and Division Two. The average age of the side was high and Crawford, at 25, was the youngest first-team regular. No wonder the rest of the country expected Town to slip quietly back whence they came.

Ramsey's unorthodox use of wingers Stephenson and Leadbetter was a major factor in the way Town upset the rhythm of more accomplished opponents. He had them playing wide on the flanks but often lying in deep positions, particularly Leadbetter. Opposing full-backs, trained to deal with wingers trying to get to the by-line, seemed confused and unable to adjust. With nobody to mark and, in those days, not required to 'overlap' themselves, they saw the game pass them by. Diagonal balls would be quickly played in to Crawford and Phillips, and the deadly duo revelled in the service. Energetic Crawford was a real handful for even the best defences, while Phillips would let fly from long range with remarkable shots of great velocity. He somehow got the heavier balls of that era to swerve and dip at high speed and one wonders how he would have fared with today's lightweight ball. His shooting caught the imagination of the *News Chronicle*, who carried out tests and measured a Phillips shot at 94mph.

Nowadays, Ramsey's tactical innovations seem simple and obvious, but in those days the traditional 'WW' 5-3-2 formation was rarely tampered with. With hindsight we can only marvel at how long it took other clubs to find a way to nullify Ipswich. The first counter-strategy to have any effect was hatched by Spurs' Bill Nicholson, but it was developed a full twelve months after Town reached the top flight.

Ramsey would develop his innovative 4-4-2 ideas further with England's so-called 'wingless wonders' during the 1966 World Cup.

Interestingly, when Ramsey was interviewed years later he had no hesitation in putting Town's championship win ahead of the World Cup triumph in his list of achievements. First Division football was generally a very open affair in 1962, with much less emphasis on tight marking and the closing down of opponents. Town won the title despite gathering a rather modest tally of 56 points (two points for a win) and despite conceding 67 goals – the worst defensive record by a Division One-winning side since 1936! There is a commonly held view that Town were a 'one season wonder' who only succeeded because of Burnley's amazing collapse. This view is bolstered by the fact that such a title triumph is unlikely ever to be repeated. The maximum wage was abolished in 1961 and within a year or two only the rich clubs could afford the top players. A 'small' club like Ipswich has not won the League in the 40 years since, and looks unlikely to do so again.

Ramsey used the same well-drilled Town eleven for virtually all of 1961-62 and was rarely hampered by injuries. In common with other clubs, he didn't build a large squad and, as it turned out, didn't need one. He dealt masterfully with an early setback when regular left-back Ken Malcolm was laid low by knee and back trouble. With no obvious replacement on the books, Ramsey turned to wing-half John Compton, who had never played at full-back. It worked like a dream, for Compton looked at home immediately and coped admirably with everything the country's best wingers could throw at him.

The smart and dignified figure of Ramsey would sit quietly alone from his vantage point next to the West Stand, taking in every move, every pass, every mistake. His impassive appearance hid a determined and single-minded attitude, and once in the dressing room he would deliver an inspiring team talk without ranting and raving, or would simply a have a quiet word in a player's ear, whichever he felt appropriate. Although they called him 'Alf', rather than 'boss', respect was immense.

His shrewd transfer dealings paid huge dividends. Few expected Leadbetter, Stephenson and Moran to be so effective in the top division, while young Baxter made a brilliant transition from Scottish junior football and coped admirably with the added pressure of having to report back for National Service duties after every game. Skipper Andy Nelson had been plucked from West Ham reserves, while keeper Bailey improved in leaps and bounds under Ramsey.

The club was proud when Crawford became its first England international, but the centre-forward aggravated an injury against Austria and had to miss Town's trip to Manchester United three days later. Skipper Nelson described the subsequent 0-5 disintegration at Old Trafford as the biggest hiding his side had ever taken. That night the championship bid looked ready to collapse. However, shortly afterwards, the penultimate game of the season proved to be an encounter Town's travelling fans will never forget. In front of 44,694 at Highbury, mighty Arsenal were completely outplayed as the deadly duo of Crawford (2) and Phillips scored the goals to set up a momentous last match for Town. It left Burnley needing maximum points from two games to pip Ipswich – and that was simply a bridge too far.

Britain in the early 1960s, viewed from a distance of 40 years, seems like another world. Although change was in the air, the average football supporter and working man viewed Prime Minister Harold Macmillan's pronouncement 'you've never had it so good' with little real enthusiasm. A life of comfort and affluence was not the lot of the typical football fan, nor was it true of the journeymen footballers of Ipswich Town.

However, things were changing and the era of the wealthy football superstar had begun to dawn. In 1961, abolition of the maximum wage had been negotiated, and the background to this footballing unrest reflected fundamental social changes. The image of the top players was evolving. In short, football had started to go 'pop'. Players like Denis Law, Derek Dougan and Johnny Haynes were being treated like showbiz stars and the stage was set for the arrival of icons like George Best. Footballers were no longer merely working class heroes, they were stars.

Despite Macmillan's radical economic modernisation programme, his government seemed crusty and out of step. The growing frustrations of the young led to satire becoming chic. Budding Oxbridge comedian Peter Cook opened a satirical nightclub in London called The Establishment and – in the same month that Town won the League – it even hosted subversive American comic Lenny Bruce. *Private Eye* produced its first scrappy editions, and the ground-breaking 'Beyond the Fringe' revue was a big hit. Meanwhile, as Ted Phillips fired his 25-yard bombs towards opposing goalkeepers, the Soviets were developing a 100-megaton missile, a project greeted with horror in the USA and which sparked a huge demo in Trafalgar Square. The erection of the Berlin Wall symbolised the stony divide between the superpowers. In the world of entertainment the energy of 1950s rock-'n'roll had fizzled out and popular music had apparently lost its edge. Even trad jazz began to prosper and Acker Bilk topped the Hit Parade in early 1962 with 'Stranger on the Shore'. The way was clear for something new and exciting, and the Beatles' first hit would come along in the autumn of 1962. Just as Ipswich Town provided a breath of fresh air in domestic soccer, so the Fab Four began to dazzle the world of showbiz. The swinging 60s had begun.

Ipswich Town chairman of the time, John Cobbold

A championship-winning forward line — Stephenson, Moran, Crawford, Phillips, Leadbetter

Goalkeeper Roy Bailey made 348 senior appearances for Ipswich Town between 1955 and 1964

Trainer-coach Jimmy Forsyth served Ipswich Town from 1950 to 1971

Chapter One

~ *Foundations* ~

1936-55

Within a year of becoming president of the amateur club Ipswich Town FC, in 1935, the aristocratic Captain J M 'Ivan' Cobbold had engineered the arrival of professional football in Suffolk's county town.

This distinguished-looking Old Etonian and former Scots Guards officer, head of the Cobbold brewing firm, had friends in high places. He took part in country sports and was a regular at royal parties at Sandringham. And it was one of his pals – Arsenal chairman Sir Samuel Hill-Wood – who first persuaded the energetic Captain to develop the potential at Ipswich Town. Sir Samuel showed him round the marble halls of Highbury and offered him all the advice and help he needed. He even made his palatial London home available to the Captain when the time came to interview candidates for the Ipswich manager's job.

In the spring of 1936, Britain's new monarch – Edward VII – was causing concern at the Foreign Office by apparently sympathising with Hitler's Germany. The King even sent the Fuhrer a birthday telegram, wishing him health and prosperity. The diplomatic skills and political awareness of Captain Cobbold that same month weren't quite so heavy-handed as he beavered behind the scenes to build a bright future for Ipswich Town. Having persuaded stubborn idealists in Ipswich that a professional club was the right way ahead, Southern League membership was quickly secured and the problem of finding a talented team-manager tackled.

The new boss was Mick O'Brien, a 42-year-old ex-Irish international, then assistant manager at Brentford and coach to the Middlesex FA. The burly and charismatic O'Brien used his contacts in the game to good effect and spent the summer assembling a squad for the huge challenge that lay ahead. Ipswich made national headlines when Scottish international Jimmy McLuckie was lured to Suffolk from Aston Villa, thanks to the offer of an attractive salary package. It was certainly a stressful time for the new manager, whose wife died shortly after his arrival in Suffolk and who had to bear the extra burden of the club secretary's duties when Len Thompson was taken ill during the hectic build-up to the new season. Hasty ground improvements were made at Portman Road, including a lick of paint and new stoves for the former cricket pavilion which served as dressing rooms.

In the week the King scandalised onlookers by setting off on a cruise with divorcee Wallis Simpson, a record 14,211 crammed into Portman Road to see the new era's opening game against Tunbridge Wells. A 4-1 win set the pattern for 1936-37, with Town going on to win the Southern League championship at the first attempt. A delighted Cobbold, buoyed by success and by the healthy crowds at home games, immediately put his club forward for election to the Football League. Town polled a healthy 24 votes, but re-election candidates Exeter and Aldershot survived by gaining 40 and 34 respectively.

This temporary setback was followed by a bombshell when the heroic figure of manager O'Brien suddenly exited the club just three weeks before the start of the 1937-38 campaign. Widower O'Brien had apparently formed an attachment with the married landlady of a local pub, a situation that his chairman found untenable, particularly as the pub was one of Cobbold's own. The Captain knew that O'Brien, despite his indiscretions, would be a hard act to follow and he aimed high when seeking a replacement. Major Frank Buckley, England's leading club manager of the era, was approached but, not surprisingly, refused to take the drop from mighty Wolves to non-League Ipswich.

The search for a new manager went on through the autumn, but this was a time when the people of Suffolk had grander matters to occupy their minds than the affairs of a minor football club. The abdication crisis that threatened the future of the monarchy was for a while focused on Ipswich. The town was in the national spotlight, for its courthouse was dealing with the Wallis Simpson divorce case. The King's sweetheart gave her address as Beach House, Felixstowe, and, after her decree nisi was granted, headlines such as 'King's Moll Reno'd in Wolsey's Home Town,' circled the world.

By early November, Captain Cobbold still hadn't found a manager of the right calibre. Desperate measures were needed. He sent a case of vintage port to the directors of Manchester United, simultaneously despatching a chauffeur-driven car to collect their manager, 49-year-old Scott Duncan, for talks. Duncan, a dapper little Scotsman, had enjoyed mixed fortunes in five years at Old Trafford. After leading the Reds to twelfth and then sixth in the Second Division, they suffered what remains the worst season in their history when relegation to the Third Division (North) in 1934 was only narrowly avoided. Duncan survived this calamity and turned things round. By 1936 United were celebrating winning the Second Division title, Duncan's reward being a new five-year contract. Relegation quickly followed, however, and despite the security of his long contract, the persuasiveness of Captain Cobbold worked its magic and prised him away from Old Trafford.

Having played for Dumbarton, Newcastle, Rangers, Celtic and Cowdenbeath, Duncan had been on a salary of £800 per annum when starting at Old Trafford, but Cobbold offered him £2,000 a year to take the Portman Road job, with a £1,000 bonus if League status could be achieved. From Old Trafford to non-League Suffolk was a huge step down but Duncan nevertheless became one of the three highest-paid managers in the land. He cut a small but immaculate figure and couldn't have been more different from his predecessor, the big, garrulous Irishman O'Brien. The new man resembled a high-ranking civil servant and, in fact, had worked for a spell in a solicitor's office before opting to stick with football. With his natty homburg, dark suit and polished shoes, Duncan commanded instant respect from the humble Suffolk-born employees at Portman Road.

With Ipswich Town having been in the temporary charge of 27-year-old assistant secretary Don Read for several months, results had been inconsistent, but Duncan reorganised things and led the side to third in the table by the end of 1937-38. Once again the club applied for Football League status. Many miles were driven in Duncan's smart new club car, a Wolseley 16, and many drinks were bought as Duncan and Cobbold worked their persuasive tongues on the men in high places at other clubs. They handed out an innovative glossy brochure which outlined Town's case for election.

Come the big day at the Football League's annual meeting in London, Cobbold mentioned to his manager that he had a feeling Town would not quite secure enough votes. The canny Scot immediately proposed a bet that Town would not only get enough votes, but would top the poll.

What Cobbold didn't fully appreciate at that point was that Duncan had recently persuaded old friends at Newcastle to vote for Town, and as a consequence five other clubs would follow the Geordie club's lead.

Town duly polled 36 votes, Walsall 34 and Gillingham 28, which meant that the Kent club would be replaced in Division Three (South) by Ipswich. Duncan's winnings – a sovereign – was duly handed over as the magnificent news was transmitted back to Suffolk. The Town party returned by train the next day to find the station and nearby streets thronged with celebrating supporters. Cobbold later addressed the massed gathering from the balcony of the Town Hall.

More ground improvements took place and the squad was further strengthened for the start of the League era. More than 19,000 crammed into Portman Road, many arriving hours before kick-off, to see the opening League game with Southend. The visitors travelled up the East Anglian coast by boat for the occasion and must have felt a little queasy as the League's new-boys cracked four goals past them, with the honour of first scorer going to Len Jones, a £150 signing from Chelmsford. That first season in the League saw Town finish a healthy seventh in the table, which to that point was the best ever debut season by newcomers.

In the New Year, Town's immaculate pitch and surrounding premises were flooded after a deluge of biblical proportions. With the first team due to play at Torquay, groundsman Freddie Blake attempted to rescue the kit-hamper by rowing down Princes Street in a coracle! He discovered that the ground's entrance was blocked by wooden sleepers, which had floated across from the terracing, so his brave efforts to retrieve the kit were foiled.

A few weeks later 19-year-old Town fan Bernard Sharp and his pal Arthur Maulden left Suffolk on their bikes at 4am on Good Friday for the 70-mile trip to Town's match at QPR. A refreshment stop was taken at Chelmsford, where milk was purchased from a roadside dairy. The hardest part of the trek saw them negotiate cobbles and tram tracks in East London before reaching Loftus Road in good time for the 2.30 kick-off. The intrepid pair were rewarded with a goalless draw. Undaunted, they cycled afterwards to stay with relatives at Gidea Park, Essex, before pedalling back to Ipswich the next morning for the afternoon game with Bristol City. Town won 4-0 and, to celebrate, the lads biked directly from the ground to Tuddenham Village Hall for the regular Saturday night 'Sixpenny Hop' event.

Ipswich Town were settling nicely into League football when life in Britain was transformed on the morning of Sunday, 3 September 1939. War with Germany was declared with just four games of the 1939-40 season completed. Cobbold announced that all football at Ipswich would be suspended until Hitler had been defeated. The angry members of Ipswich Town Supporters' Association – England's largest such organisation, boasting some 10,000 members – wrote to complain! The Home Office and football authorities soon relaxed their blanket ban, to permit friendlies, but Cobbold took a harder line. He issued a second statement on 30 September, announcing the closure of Portman Road. Ipswich thus became the first League club to officially shut its gates for the duration of the war. The club's 35 players were given their cards and allowed to collect their boots, while club kit and other effects were taken for storage at the Cobbold brewery. Manager Duncan was put on a retainer, but found himself a post at Churchman's cigarette factory next to the ground. Some of the players also took jobs at Churchman's, and others at the brewery.

By 1943, Cobbold, who had by that time risen to the rank of lieutenant-colonel, reported a financial crisis at the mothballed football club. Its accounts showed debts of over £14,000 and the directors chipped in to meet the demands of creditors, Cobbold himself having to find over £11,000. A year later, the club's inspirational leader was dead, aged just 47. In June 1944 he had attended a service at the Guards Chapel in London when it was hit by a German flying bomb. He was one of several victims to lose their lives. He left a widow, Lady Blanche, who would go on to play a prominent role at her late husband's beloved club. Lady Blanche was the second daughter of the ninth Duke of Devonshire, and sister-in-law of future Prime Minister Harold Macmillan. The couple had four children, and both sons – Patrick and John – would follow their father and become chairmen of Ipswich Town.

A combination of the war and the loss of their charismatic chairman inevitably slowed Ipswich Town's rapid rise from obscurity. Although the conflict with Germany ended in May 1945, that with Japan still had no end in sight, and might have had years to run but for the atomic bombs dropped on Hiroshima and Nagasaki in August.

And with fuel still rationed, circumstances would not permit a return to normal League football until August 1946. The first post-war season, 1945-46, was therefore 'unofficial'. The Third Division (South) was split into a southern and northern section. Ipswich competed in the northern, with ten others. The new era began with a new man in the chair, in the shape of Philip Cobbold, uncle of the late Captain Ivan. Philip found himself running both the brewery business and football club, despite suffering a recent heart attack. The burden on his health proved too heavy and he died at Christmas 1945. Philip Cobbold was succeeded as chairman at Portman Road by the managing director of Fisons, Peter Chevallier.

To allow clubs to get back on their feet after the enforced break, the League continued the wartime practice of permitting guest appearances by players who were engaged in National Service locally. This enabled some experienced men to be drafted into the Town side, although occasionally their commitment to the cause was loudly questioned from the terraces. A happier reception awaited one new recruit, dapper inside-forward Tommy Parker, who scored twice on his debut to mark the start of a 30-year association with the club. He would go on to set a club appearances record before taking charge of the development office, a precursor of the modern marketing department.

Transport problems regularly reared their head during this transitional season. For the trip to Clapton Orient, Ipswich's team bus spluttered to a halt beside the A12 at Stratford St Mary. A passing van driver was persuaded to take the players to London for a small cash consideration. At the conclusion of the temporary 'mini-league', which ended before Christmas, Town finished sixth. The same teams all played each other again after the turn of the year, but now the fixtures were designated part of the Division Three (South) northern section cup. Football, of course, was one of the few entertainments on offer for the working man during this period of post-war austerity, meaning attendances were high everywhere. Grounds were often bursting at the seams, and at a Bolton v Stoke FA Cup-tie 60,000 squeezed into Burnden Park. When more tried to join them, a wall collapsed resulting in 33 deaths and 500 injuries. Ipswich made a donation to the disaster fund and a collection among fans realised a further sum.

If the first post-war season was truncated by circumstance, the second, 1946-47 – which saw the restoration of the Football League –

would become the longest on record. Midweek games were banned in a bid to maintain high industrial production. This, added to the havoc caused by one of the worst winters on record, necessitated so many postponements that the League season did not run its course until mid-June.

Gates soared, and even Town reserves pulled in over 10,000 for a match with Arsenal. As if further encouragement was needed, the Government decreed that admission to all grounds should be reduced from 1s 6d (7.5p) to 1s 3d.

A key man in the Ipswich defence by this time was skipper Matt O'Mahony, but the 33-year-old must have questioned his value to the side after a troubled weekend visit to Brighton. When the team's bus was involved in its second traffic accident en route, O'Mahony got off to buy a paper, only to find on his return the party had left without him. The following day a gale tore apart Portman Road's East Stand, the roof deposited in the nearby cattle market.

Town finished 1946-47 in a highly satisfactory sixth place. The following campaign, which was interrupted by another hostile winter, saw them improve to fourth, a position which would have been even better had they not lost their last three games. O'Mahony had demanded a transfer when he and his new bride could not find a suitable house in the area. Manager Duncan bemoaned the lack of unfurnished property available, but the Supporters' Association saved the day by purchasing a handsome property in Christchurch Street specifically for renting to players from outside the area.

This was one of many ways in which Duncan and his side were assisted by loyal and devoted fans. One such character was Ron Ellis, a locally born bachelor whose quiet and humble nature hid an astonishing memory for Ipswich Town minutiae. Ron watched his first Ipswich game in 1935, beginning a close association with the club which would last until his death 65 years later. Ron began helping the club by taking the players' boots to a cobbler friend for repair, and by ferrying the club's outgoing mail to the Post Office every day. When the team travelled by rail, Ron would taxi players home and make sure the team skip got back to Portman Road safely. He was trusted and liked by several generations of staff and players and would provide hours of entertainment with his remarkable feats of memory. Even well into his retirement years, Ron could recall facts and figures about any Town match from the past, however long ago. If anyone threw a random date at him – maybe their birth-date – he would put his head into his hands while he clicked his brain into gear. Half a minute or so later he would reveal on which day of the week that date had fallen, and how Town had fared in the game nearest to it. His skills had more practical uses, too, as for many years he would compile statistics for the *East Anglian Daily Times* reporters to use in their match previews. Ron died in March 2000 after 65 years of devotion to Ipswich Town, whereupon his ashes were scattered on the Portman Road pitch. Chairman David Sheepshanks described him as 'our greatest fan and a fantastic servant'.

Town began 1948-49 in grand style, hammering sixteen goals in their first three games, but shortly afterwards tumbled to a record 2-9 defeat at Tommy Lawton-inspired Notts County. By this time, a new signature tune – 'Here Comes The Town' – was introduced to accompany the players' arrival on the pitch, but due to popular demand the traditional 'Entry of the Gladiators' was soon restored, ultimately surviving until the 1980s. Town spent most of the season in mid-table, ultimately finishing seventh, but the average age of its players was higher than that at most clubs. Duncan addressed this problem by targetting South Wales in a search for new young talent and signed up Dai Rees and John Elsworthy as a result. Another new face at the club was John Cobbold, at 21 the youngest director in the country.

The 1949-50 season proved to be a massive disappointment, with goals hard to come by and lowly status throughout. New record signing Sammy McCrory became the first Town player to be sent off in the League in a bad-tempered 0-5 hammering at Aldershot. Burly inside-forward Elsworthy recalled his Ipswich debut, as a teenager in December 1949:

'I reduced the average age of the side considerably. Only Tommy Parker was under 30, with the eldest being 41. I remember in those days we would get a new ball for first-team games and this was used by the reserves the following Saturday, and then for training after that. We were given one pair of boots and one pair of training shoes and these were expected to last for three years! In 1952 we played Bournemouth in an FA Cup replay at Arsenal and took the opportunity to peek into the Highbury boot-room. Their players had three pairs of boots each – we couldn't believe it.'

Poor results in early 1950 prompted several departures. Coach George Smith paid the price for being publicly critical in a newspaper article of his manager and board, while chairman Chevallier stepped down due to pressure of work, to be replaced by Alistair Cobbold. Smith had been seen as an innovative coach and was ruthless in his bid to get Town's ageing and overweight squad fit. One of his new ideas was to stage coaching sessions for local schoolboys. One eager lad who attended these was Brian Cant, who later recalled being picked for a select squad of 30 boys, only to find himself cast back into football oblivion by George Smith's ignominious departure. Cant would later find fame as TV presenter of 'Playschool', 'Playaway' and 'Dramarama' and voice-over artist on children's shows 'Trumpton' and 'Camberwick Green'.

Among Town's keenest fans during this era were schoolboys Mick Banthorpe – later to play for the 'A' team and reserves – and his pal David Hicks. Recalls Mick: 'When David and I were eight years old we both asked for Ipswich Town football kits for Christmas. In those days you simply couldn't buy replica kits though, and our two mums gallantly trekked all over town, finally coming up with royal blue rugby shirts and white shorts that came over our knees. After unwrapping our presents bright and early on Christmas morning we disappeared in the new kit into Christchurch Park straight after breakfast and didn't return until my sister fetched us back for Christmas dinner.

'I also remember dodging school with a couple of mates one afternoon to go to an FA Cup replay. Our punishment after being found out was missing the Christmas school play. After beating Norwich one time, a small group of us left Carrow Road taunting the opposition by singing 'Have you heard the death of poor Cock Robin?' More and more joined in until it reached a crescendo. It was stirring stuff for us youngsters – but it was good-natured and there wasn't a punch or a bottle thrown. When I was a bit older I had the privilege of running out at Portman Road as a 14-year-old after being picked for the Ipswich Schools team. 'Entry of the Gladiators' blared out of the speakers, just like it did for the first team, and that really brought out the goose pimples!'

Town improved in 1950-51, with their final resting place of eighth representing good progress after a poor start. Jimmy Forsyth, nicknamed 'Chisel' because of his prominent chin, arrived as trainer from

Millwall. He would go on to serve the club for 21 years and around 1,000 games. That season saw Town do the double over League newcomers and neighbours Colchester, while local recruit David Deacon made a name for himself by playing full-back for the 'A' team, reserves and first team within just eight days. The goalkeeper at the start of 1951-52 was Len Burns, starting his 25th year in pro football at the advanced age of 43. His and everyone else's season petered out in disappointing fashion as Town finished seventeenth, although they continued to build a nationwide reputation for the magnificent condition of the Portman Road pitch. During the February home match with Plymouth, a minute's silence was observed and the national anthem played to mark the death of King George VI.

The following season produced an identical points haul of 41, and a slightly better finishing position of sixteenth. Among Town's preseason signings was Ossie Higgins, a former international boxer, from Aston Villa. Higgins managed few first-team games at Portman Road, however, and, after being released, returned to boxing. He won a silver medal at the 1958 Empire Games, losing the Light Heavyweight final narrowly to an Australian. John Elsworthy remembers Higgins as 'a player you would want on your side in training'. Elsworthy himself had a fine season in 1952-53 and was watched closely by scouts from Liverpool and elsewhere. Lacklustre events on the field were overshadowed by the east coast floods of early 1953, the most catastrophic British weather event of the century. A total of 307 people lost their lives and the damage was appalling. The River Gipping overflowed and Portman Road was submerged under three feet of water. A pump was needed to rid the Main Stand enclosure of water and some fish were spotted enjoying this new aquatic environment. The Ipswich team arrived back from their game at Torquay at the height of the floods and found themselves marooned at Ipswich railway station for hours.

In early 1953 Sheffield Wednesday's dynamic young forward Derek Dooley sustained a badly broken leg in a match at Preston. Gangrene set in and the limb had to be amputated, thus ending a promising career. It was suggested at the time that bacteria in the Deepdale soil had infected Dooley's leg, and Ipswich players were relieved they'd been given routine tetanus injections some months earlier. The Dooley episode was still fresh in people's minds when Town full-back

David Deacon broke his leg against Millwall. The St John Ambulance team who treated Deacon were afterwards criticised in letters to the local press, which accused them of a lack of alertness in attending the stricken player. This had prompted his worried team-mates to 'hasten them along'.

In the summer of 1953 director John Cobbold loaned a group of players his Land Rover to get to a charity cricket match in Norfolk, but on their return the vehicle was involved in an accident, as a result of which the four men inside sustained minor injuries. Ironically, manager Duncan had already banned his players from owning cars as he felt they were dangerous and expensive luxuries. The board approved the ban on players, but insisted that Duncan own a car himself, apparently because they feared he would otherwise submit huge taxi and train expenses. Ted Pole, who was one of the Land Rover passengers, regularly used a motorcycle to get to training in those days, but chose to park it away from the ground so his manager wouldn't get the chance to rebuke him.

1953-54 got off to a fine start with four straight wins. Duncan's signing of Billy Reed, George McLuckie and Alex Crowe transformed Town from a moderate outfit into title-chasers who played attractive football. The team clinched the Division Three (South) championship, earning a civic reception and a tour of the town that eclipsed even the celebrations of 1938. Perhaps Town's luck changed with the arrival at Portman Road of a seven-leaf clover, which Duncan mounted on his office wall. It had been presented by an American airman in return for a four-leaf clover that Duncan's wife had given to American golfer Sam Snead, before he won the British Open several years earlier.

The lucky clover took pride of place in an office that was decidedly modest even by 1954 standards. The building, positioned to the left of the Churchman's Stand, was an old Nissen hut which had seen lively service during the war. It was covered in bullet indentations and was a draughty, leaky place. It had tiny windows of frosted glass strengthened by chicken wire, and the interior was divided up by flimsy wooden partitions with coconut matting on the floor.

Once promotion was secured, Duncan – a painfully slow one-fingered typist – decided he would need secretarial help, now that Town were big shots in the Second Division. He was reluctant to advertise, for fear of attracting under-qualified young ladies interested only in the 'glamour' of football, so he shared his problem with his bank manager at Lloyd's. The bank manager duly informed his own staff that Ipswich Town were looking for an able typist with shorthand skills, at which one of the young tellers pricked up her ears. She knew a friend with exactly the right qualifications, who happened to be a keen Town supporter and had expressed privately a desire to work for the club. The friend in question was 19-year-old Patricia Godbold, who'd been hooked on football since being taken along by her father seven years earlier. Pat jumped at the opportunity presented before her. She recalled: 'I went and saw Mr Duncan and he hired me without seeing anyone else. He warned me I'd have to keep an eye out for the players though, especially the married ones!'

Females on the staff were a new phenomenon at Portman Road and for young Pat's comfort the club quickly had a ladies' toilet cubicle built out of breeze blocks. She still remembers with a shiver the chilly walk outside to her private convenience. Meanwhile, back inside the Nissen hut: 'We always knew when Mr Duncan had finished work at the end of the day, for we'd hear him banging his large glass Cobbold ashtray on the window ledge to empty out the cigarette ends. They would go all over the coke and coal that was piled up outside.' The office area and wooden dressing rooms may have been spartan, but they would serve the club until 1965, when smart new premises were finally created on the same corner of the ground.

Pat went on to work at Portman Road for 43 years (serving nine different managers) and still had part-time duties there in 2002. She was not the only new face from the spring of 1954. A highly promising player called Edward Phillips had been discovered 'out in the sticks' of rural Suffolk. Recently returned from National Service in Malaya, young Ted was a fast, strong forward with a fierce shot. After spending his weekends banging in goals for Leiston Town and his weekdays 'working' the local forests with his ferrets, Ipswich offered him an alternative way of making a living. But more of Ted later.

Joining the Second Division in 1954 for the first time, Town saw fit to carry out only a few minor ground improvements and make just two low-key signings. With hindsight, their preparations were woefully inadequate. A four-match winning start was followed by ten straight defeats and they slid to the bottom of the table. A mini-revival in the spring of 1955 came too late to prevent the bitter pill of relegation.

Billy Baxter played 459 senior games for Ipswich Town between 1960 and 1971

Defensive stalwarts Roy Bailey, Larry Carberry, Andy Nelson, John Elsworthy and John Compton

Alf Ramsey and some players' wives at a club function

Chapter Two

~ *Ramsey at the Helm* ~

1955-60

While the Soviet Union and the creation of the Warsaw Pact made headlines in May 1955, some of the back pages were reporting the resignation of a Scot who eighteen years earlier had joined Ipswich Town on a mission to steer them into the Football League. Manager Scott Duncan, now 67, decided it was time to make way for new blood at Portman Road. Relegation after just one season in Division Two proved that Town had been ill-prepared for the bigger stage and Duncan was content for a new, younger man to try his luck.

Duncan agreed with the board that he would relinquish control of the team when a new man was found, but stay on as club secretary. Town director Nat Rowe, owner of the local greyhound stadium, alerted his colleagues to the likely availability of former England full-back Alf Ramsey as Duncan's replacement. Ramsey, now 35, was out in the cold at Spurs, having lost his first-team place and being omitted from a close-season tour. The Cobbolds always did things in the proper manner and Spurs were formally approached for permission to speak to Ramsey. However, the player had just set off on a nine-week FA coaching stint in Rhodesia, and talks had to be delayed.

As news leaked out that Ramsey was Ipswich's target, Duncan continued to supervise the summer search for new players. He recruited a fellow ageing Scot in inside-forward Jimmy Leadbetter of Brighton. Leadbetter saw the move as a means of getting a house for his family, who were unhappy in their flat on the south coast. The local press introduced him to Town fans as a ball player who was on the frail side, but full of pluck and never likely to shirk a tackle. Meanwhile, one that got away was the splendidly named Idris Niblett, a talented youngster at Barry Town. After terms had been agreed with Ipswich, Niblett unexpectedly joined Cardiff for a bigger fee. The episode led to resignations at Barry and a row over underhand dealings.

The summer of 1955 proved to be one of intrigue. Shortly after Ruth Ellis went to the gallows for murdering her lover, entering history as the last woman ever to be hanged in Britain, Ipswich Town fans got in a lather over the famous footballer who arrived for talks at Portman Road wearing a smart England blazer and accompanied by his pretty young wife. The appointment of 35-year-old Alf Ramsey as Town's new manager was announced soon afterwards, but it was made clear he had no intention of playing. Asked if he would take control of training, he replied: 'Oh no, I'll leave that to the trainer, but I am a young man and feel I might be able to help.' He was delighted by the excellent Portman Road playing surface, which he called a 'a real beauty'. Ramsey was by no means the first to praise a pitch that was lovingly nurtured by little Freddie Blake and his assistant, Stanley Prendergast, and which was the envy of many big clubs.

Ramsey is so central to subsequent events covered in this book that it is worth examining his background in detail. Born in the rural outskirts of Dagenham in 1920, he was one of four sons of Albert and Florence Ramsey. Hard-working Albert operated a small-holding in the week and drove a dustcart on Saturdays. Alf and his brothers played football on a meadow behind their home and used to dribble and pass a tennis ball along their four-mile walk to and from school.

The Ramseys' end of town was green and rural, but the building of the huge Beacontree housing estate and the arrival of the Ford Motor Company in 1929 saw Dagenham transformed from a country hamlet to a London suburb within a very short time. Alf, nicknamed 'Darkie', proved to be a useful young footballer, and rose to become captain of his school team, later of Dagenham Schools, then of Essex Schools. After failing to find work at Ford, he was taken on by the local Co-op grocery store and was glad to be earning twelve shillings a week as Britain struggled through the 1930s' depression.

The owner of a local sweet shop noticed that lads like Alf had spare time on their hands and formed the Five Elms United side to occupy them. Grocery assistant Ramsey was already a composed and steady player and soon attracted the attention of a scout working for Portsmouth. In those pre-war days, the 88 League clubs employed 1,000 professionals but the naturally cautious Alf doubted his chances of a career in the game. After much persuasion he apparently signed forms proffered by the persistent scout, but was then disappointed when he heard no more from Fratton Park.

Called to arms in 1940, Ramsey did infantry training at Truro, St Austell and then Barton Stacey in Hampshire. He cut a strapping, if rather slow-moving, figure and was made captain of the battalion football team. In 1943 that team played Southampton at The Dell in a pre-season friendly and not long afterwards the Saints invited him to make up the numbers for their war-depleted first team. This led to the offer of a professional contract, but again he took his time signing, initially doubting he could make the grade.

One wartime fixture saw him net four goals as an inside-forward against Luton, but his neat and tidy style of play, allied to a lack of pace, clearly marked him down as a defender, and this became his pre-ferred role. After a six-month posting to Palestine he was demobbed in June 1946 and invited back to The Dell. After more prolonged negotiations his progress was hastened when manager Bill Dodgin suggested he try playing at right-back. As a plodding perfectionist this was ideal for Ramsey, and after a tentative start his career got proper-ly under way at the age of nearly 27.

England did not have an embarrassment of riches at right-back, and before long Ramsey was called into the national squad. He played against Switzerland 'B', but at the final whistle reporters interested in the views of this 'Johnny come lately' were politely turned away. FA regulations did not permit players to speak to the press. This situation persisted for years and, as a creature of habit, and a shy man to boot, this 'enforced' silence became hard for Alf to break.

In his book, *Talking Football*, Ramsey revealed: 'I have found that serious reading has helped me develop a command of words so essen-tial when you suddenly find yourself being called upon to make a speech. People, remember, are inclined to forget that speech-making may not be your strong point.' Wrestling with the PR side of being a club captain, Ramsey became ever more self-conscious about his East London accent, acutely aware that perfect BBC enunciation was seen as the ideal in those days.

Regular England call-ups saw the *Daily Mail* describe Ramsey as 'looking suave and cool as a city businessman' in his country's No 2 shirt. However, things went sour at Southampton and, after a March 1949 transfer request was granted, he moved to Spurs for £21,000 – a record fee for a full-back, although it included a player-exchange – Ernie Jones moving to The Dell as a makeweight.

The transfer to White Hart Lane enabled Ramsey to return to his family home in Dagenham. He did well in Arthur Rowe's 'push and run' Spurs side and was part of England's 1950 World Cup campaign in Brazil. He was in the side that suffered the humiliating 0-1 defeat by the USA. Although the England team were clearly stuck in a time-warp, Spurs were tactical innovators at the time and Ramsey became a key figure for them. Spurs men would seek to hold the ball for a minimum of time, attempting to keep it on the ground and pushing it ahead into space for colleagues to run on to. As part of this scheme, Ramsey effectively became one of the very first attacking wing-backs. In those pre-TV days, new tactical systems could retain their shock value for much longer than would be the case today and, at Ipswich, Ramsey would later exploit this to maximum advantage.

Ramsey's 32nd and final cap for England was the 3-6 debacle against Hungary at Wembley in 1953. Both Ramsey and manager Walter Winterbottom were ridiculed afterwards for making lame excuses for the result. Their attitude came over as ill-judged and short-sighted – for England had clearly been outclassed.

During the 1954-55 season Spurs signed the dynamic young Danny Blanchflower, the upshot of which was that Ramsey was dropped for the first time. Clearly, his playing days were nearly over. He was by now 35, although still widely thought to be 33. This misunderstanding came about because his birthday was published as being in 1922 – an error he chose not to correct, presumably because it helped him win better contracts at Southampton and Spurs. Later, much was made of this 'deception', and his biographers, Dave Bowler and Max Marquis, both concluded that he actively encouraged the deceit. His true birth-date would subsequently come to light in Debrett's, after he was knighted in 1967.

After Spurs had been humiliated in the FA Cup by Third Division York City, major changes swept through White Hart Lane. In addition to the arrival of Blanchflower, manager Rowe had what amounted to a nervous breakdown. The ageing Ramsey was overlooked to the extent that he was not even invited on a close-season tour to Hungary. There was also no indication of a coaching role for him, as he had been led to believe. Ramsey didn't hang around to argue the toss and headed to Rhodesia to get himself some coaching experience.

For Ramsey, the end of the line had clearly been reached at White Hart Lane, and the enquiries from managerless Ipswich were both flattering and timely. Ipswich's rural location and its slower pace of life attracted Ramsey, but the move surprised some of his old team-mates. George Robb felt he'd been shabbily treated by Tottenham: 'I was surprised he went to Ipswich because at the time they were nothing really, and they didn't seem to have too much potential.'

Ramsey quickly discovered that he had little raw material to work with at Portman Road. He said he had no preconceived ideas how he was going to ask his new team to play, but would decide tactics after seeing what he'd inherited. It was a rude awakening for a man who'd just spent five years in football's top echelons. The annual pre-season public practice match at Portman Road was far from a show-stopper. Admission was three shillings for the best seats and a shilling for the terraces, to watch the first team attack line up against the first choice defence. Played in pouring rain – which kept the crowd below 5,000 – the action was so insipid that wife Vickie tugged Ramsey's sleeve at half-time and urged him to go home.

Ramsey's chose his words carefully after this match, but seemed to acknowledge the lack of quality: 'The main thing that struck me was that there seems to be very little difference between a good many of the players.' Less than a fortnight after arriving, Ramsey took charge of the 1955-56 season's curtain-raiser and sat impassively through a depressing 0-2 home defeat by Torquay. Slow-handclapping from the terraces greeted Town's disjointed performance. Wisely, Ramsey didn't panic and said there was no point in immediately axing anyone as, if he did this, there would have to be seven or eight victims!

His first task was to organise his defence, and this was done quickly and effectively. Players like Neil Myles, modestly talented but efficient and focused, responded well to Ramsey's methods. Results soon improved and the directors – having slashed wages in the wake of relegation – now raised the players' weekly pay to £15, with a £2 win bonus. This meant they were earning nearly double the national average wage of the time.

Before long Ramsey quietly enrolled himself for elocution lessons in Ipswich, apparently believing his East London accent was inappropriate, now that he was moving in managerial circles. Although this was denied by Ramsey himself, John Eastwood, a young fan in those days, who later co-wrote a detailed history of the club, confirms: 'It was well known that Alf took himself off for two-hour elocution lessons to a woman at the ballroom dancing school near Barrack Corner.'

Ramsey's newly cultivated voice, with its clipped and studied tones, presumably gave him the confidence and authority he needed, and made him more at ease when mingling with the aristocratic Cobbold family and the other blue blood directors. However, the new voice struck many as slightly odd and would leave him wide open to lampooning. Supporters of today who never saw a Ramsey interview could perhaps refer to boxer Chris Eubank as a modern equivalent – minus the lisp and monocle. Ramsey's expressionless and leaden-paced delivery, out of barely moving lips, made him sound cold and impassive, like a man desperate to say the right thing, the right way. At worst it came over as pretentious, and at best slightly pompous.

Although he ridded himself of his working class accent, his syntax was still mangled. Recent managers such as Ron Atkinson and Dave Bassett are also guilty of this but, unlike those two, Ramsey exuded little charm or charisma. He sprinkled his sentences with 'in respect of', 'in terms of', 'in as much as', but the effect was ruined when he continued to drop the 'g' off words that ended with '-ing'. Max Marquis later wrote that Ramsey in front of a microphone reminded him of King George VI announcing the opening of the Festival of Britain, bravely battling through his embarrassing stammer.

On the field of play, Town's players soon began doing their manager's talking for him. Rock'n'roll arrived in the autumn of 1955, when Bill Haley's 'Rock Around The Clock' soared up the charts, and Ipswich had also danced up the League table by the turn of the year. A crucial development took place shortly after Christmas when Ramsey decided to try Leadbetter as a deep-lying winger.

Having up to that point been in and out of the side, the spindly inside-forward was surprised to be asked to play outside-left, particularly as he was conspicuously short of pace. But Ramsey asked him to hang back and not worry about heading for the by-line. Instead, he should concentrate on picking up the ball and passing it quickly and accurately from deep. Leadbetter was given the No 11 shirt for the trip to Northampton and the experiment paid instant dividends. Town hammered the Cobblers 5-0, then repeated that scoreline at Millwall a few weeks later. By now, memories of the awful opening day had disappeared and the promotion chase was well and truly on.

When goalkeeper Charlie Ashcroft broke his arm in a reserve game, Ramsey beat the transfer deadline to recruit Roy Bailey from

Crystal Palace. The 26-year-old was living in a humble caravan at the time, but his arrival at Portman Road caused a sensation among his new team-mates, who thought a real 'big-time Charlie' had arrived. Regally driving past their bicycles, Bailey swept into the ground in a smart Ford Prefect, bearing personalised registration plates. Ramsey's secretary, Pat Godbold explains: 'Roy was the first player to have his own car, as the previous manager [Duncan] hadn't allowed it. But this rule was nothing to do with Alf, so he didn't have a problem over Roy's car. The other players mostly had bikes and were really impressed, especially by the number plate ROY 661. Roy's brother had spotted this vehicle and its number plate and had tipped him off, so Roy went out and bought it.'

Dark-haired Bailey was born in Surrey, the fifth child in a family of thirteen. He proved a dependable and inspirational custodian, with great agility. Tall, but not particularly heavily built, he went on to become a highly popular figure. During his time in Suffolk, his son Gary was born, later to play between the sticks for Manchester United and England. Bailey made his debut in the local derby at Norwich over Easter 1956, along with inside-forward Doug Millward. With Town chasing promotion, the travelling fans were horrified to see the Canaries go two up before the two new boys had even touched the ball. The game ended 3-2 in City's favour and Town subsequently missed promotion by just two points. Things might have been different had Ramsey's men not been hampered by injuries. At one stage no fewer than six men were in plaster.

Scott Duncan, as club secretary, was still at the ground every day and, although Ramsey was in sole charge of the team, he wasn't entirely happy about his predecessor's presence on the fringe of things. The matter came to a head after Charlton Athletic made a bid for Ramsey's services. Ramsey would be staying, said the board, and Duncan would take more of a back-seat role. By the summer of 1956 Ramsey had familiarised himself with the Suffolk non-league scene. He travelled to Bury St Edmunds to capture full-back Larry Carberry, an ex-sheet metal worker, based in the town with the King's Regiment. He also brought back Ted Phillips from Stowmarket, where the forward had spent the previous season on loan. Even with these new faces available, 1956-57 got off to a poor start and Town were bottom after seven games. However, the corner was dramatically turned when first

Coventry and then Brentford were hammered 4-0 within a few days of each other. The latter game saw rejuvenated Town score twice in the first 50 seconds, a Football League record.

With skipper and long-serving Tommy Parker laid low by injury, Phillips was given the No 10 shirt and soon began banging in the goals. Strong and quick, poker-faced Phillips was a real rough diamond, with a reputation for being something of a tearaway as a youngster. Earlier in his Town career there were doubts about his future as a professional, so Town released him temporarily to Stowmarket, while keeping an eye on his progress and retaining his League registration.

John Eastwood recalls: 'During that one season Ted hit dozens of goals for Stowmarket, so Ramsey got him back again, and overlooked his past misdemeanours. When he was a kid, Ted apparently fell down a deep well near his home in Leiston and nearly drowned. His mum had to fish him out by lowering the bucket. He scraped his head badly in this incident and this caused the distinctive patch on the back of his head. He was a dressing room joker, wearing wigs and playing practical jokes. He was big and rangy but a lot of people forget that he scored very few headers – nearly all his goals were down to his shooting ability.'

Phillips would make a name for himself with his astonishing shooting. Leadbetter recalled: 'With the lighter balls they play with nowadays, Ted could have scored from the halfway line, because he could hit a ball! He didn't always know where it was going himself, he put such a swerve on it.' Phillips always did a little shuffle before unleashing a shot, which was a dead giveaway, but usually he had time and space because he'd run into the space created by winger Leadbetter's 'absence'. Phillips' natural strength and power with a ball would also serve him well on the cricket field, for he became a feared pace bowler with Colchester and East Essex CC and Minor Counties side Suffolk.

From time to time Phillips suffered dramatic dips in form and under any other manager one suspects his career might have been shorter and less celebrated. Ramsey handled him carefully and with great patience. The office staff at Portman Road recall with amusement an early morning ritual involving these two men, who were like chalk and cheese. As Phillips travelled to training from his Colchester home by rail, he invariably arrived earlier than his team-mates. To kill time, he would sit in a corner of the club offices and quietly read his paper. Every morning Ramsey would arrive and stride past and say 'Morning Ted'. From behind the *Daily Mirror*, came the reply 'Morning Alf'. Always the same, every day for years. Phillips' emergence in 1956 was timely, for Parker's back injury forced him to quit at the age of 33 and Town would also temporarily lose the services of Tom Garneys. That season Phillips equalled Derek Dooley's post-war record of 41 League goals. It propelled Town toward the top of the table and a three-way battle for the title with Torquay and Colchester.

The autumn of 1956 saw the world hover on the edge of a major conflagration. The Suez Crisis saw Prime Minister Anthony Eden resign, eventually to be replaced by Harold Macmillan, the uncle of Town's youngest director, John Cobbold. At the height of the crisis, Town created a diplomatic incident of their own during an FA Cup home tie with Fulham. Losing 2-3, the players reacted badly when a late Town 'equaliser' was ruled out. Referee Ken Stokes ruled that the final whistle had sounded a split-second before the ball hit the net. Even the normally dignified Ramsey stormed into the referee's room afterwards. Although he accepted the subsequent explanation from Mr Stokes, a howling mob hung around outside chanting 'we want the ref'. This menacing behaviour by supporters led to the club receiving a ticking off from the FA.

On the final day of the season Town needed a win at Southampton to become champions and gain promotion, as long as Torquay didn't win at struggling Crystal Palace. Returning to his old stomping ground, Ramsey inspired a 2-0 defeat of the Saints. Then came a tense wait for the Torquay result. Leadbetter remembered: 'Afterwards we sat in the dressing room, waiting for Torquay's result to come through, because they'd kicked off about 45 minutes after we had. It was terrible, we had all these rumours coming through that Torquay had won, then we found out it was a draw. We went up on goal-average. Coming home, getting near Ipswich, the train driver was pulling the whistle all the way, and we had a great reception.' A few weeks later Macmillan made his famous speech at Bedford, telling the nation they'd 'never had it so good'. Celebrating Town fans were inclined to agree.

It was Town's second Third Division (South) shield in four years and this time the club was determined to prepare itself better for the higher level of football. The first major change came in the board-room, where John Cobbold replaced his cousin Alistair and became the League's youngest chairman at 29. The son of the legendary Captain Ivan, 'Mr John' would remain at the helm until 1976. A cheer-ful, outgoing character, he treated football as fun and loved to share a joke with the players, who responded warmly after overcoming their initial reticence to his plummy accent. He expected commitment from his manager and players, but not miracles. Officials from other clubs looked forward to the Cobbold hospitality. He cut an Oscar Wilde fig-ure, spouting one-liners such as: 'The only crisis at Ipswich Town is when the white wine runs out.'

Broadcaster David Coleman wrote: 'John Cobbold is perhaps the youngest chairman in the League, but also one of the wisest. He and his directors let the manager manage, and the result is satisfactory to all. Don't think, however, the board is comprised of a lot of hayseeds just because Ipswich is not a big city.'

Two years before becoming Town chairman, Cobbold narrowly lost out when fighting the Ipswich seat for the Conservatives in the 1955 General Election. He was beaten by Labour's Richard Stokes, who'd held the seat since prising it from the Tories' grip in 1938. When Stokes died in 1957, Cobbold tried again in the subsequent by-election, only to see the red majority increased by Dingle Foot (broth-er of Michael), newly defected from the Liberals. Doomed not to fol-low in the footsteps of two other Cobbolds who'd represented Ipswich many years earlier, he took his rejection badly – particularly as his strong local connections had given him better credentials than Foot, who was painted as a carpet-bagging outsider.

Nevertheless, Cobbold remained at the heart of the town's busi-ness and social scene, tackling his Ipswich Town role with gusto and heading up the brewery that was first established on Ipswich's Cliff Quay in 1746. A merger with fellow East Anglian brewers Tollemache went ahead in 1957, and Tolly Cobbold was born.

In the autumn of 1957, as Ipswich Town embarked on their sec-ond attempt to conquer the Second Division, the world was a fast-changing place. The first space satellite, Sputnik, was launched by the Soviet Union, and was followed a month later by Sputnik 2, carrying the dog Laika. The writings of beat generation icons like Jack Kerouac and Allen Ginsberg gained major recognition and coffee bars began springing up in all the hippest places. However, as far as Ipswich players were concerned, Jim Thangamunny's 'greasy spoon' in Princes Street was the only place to be after training.

Major work had been carried out in the summer to construct a new West Stand at Portman Road. It was flanked by two large white wooden observation posts, which would be occupied on matchdays by manager Ramsey and by the hospital radio team and tannoy announcer. For much of 1957-58 Town found themselves without sharpshooter Phillips, victim of a knee injury, but dependable veteran Garneys took on the mantle of leading marksman and helped the team to a highly respectable eighth place. Town put up a stirring fight in the FA Cup before losing to Manchester United. It turned out to be the last home appearance at Old Trafford for the Busby Babes, soon to suffer the Munich air crash. Scott Duncan, who lost personal friends in the disaster, was one of the Town party who attended a memorial service for the victims.

Ramsey took on the title of secretary-manager when Duncan, now 69, decided to leave the club at the end of 1957-58 to return to his native Scotland. Ramsey acquired extra office duties, but also the absolute control of day-to-day affairs that he had always craved. Soon after 1958-59 got under way, Ramsey signed energetic 22-year-old centre-forward Ray Crawford from Portsmouth for £5,000. Crawford seized his chance when Dermot Curtis was away on Republic of Ireland international duty. Crawford scored twice on his debut and never looked back, missing just two games and finishing leading scorer. He recalled: 'When I first went there, that system Alf had wasn't so obvious, but when I got into the side you saw the wingers dropping deeper. I don't think he quite had the players he wanted to play that system and my going there was part of the change towards that. He'd got Jimmy Leadbetter already but he had to build gradually. He brought in some others like Roy Stephenson later and it all seemed to fall into place.'

Town's form fell away after Christmas 1958 and they eventually finished sixteenth. Ramsey took flak for not signing a partner for Crawford in the absence of Garneys and the again-injured Phillips. The manager kept faith with Phillips and was content to wait for his return. In the summer of 1959 he surprised many by flatly rejecting a substantial bid by Liverpool for the player.

After a miserable start to 1959-60, Town's form warmed up as the winter drew in and the decade came to a close. A run of six straight wins at the close of 1959 had the fans dreaming of promotion to the top flight. It was a good time to be a Town fan and John Eastwood remembers: 'In the late 50s there was always a steady stream of fans changing ends at the interval to be at the end Town were attacking. Later the North Stand acquired a reputation for yobbishness, but at the age of sixteen it was considered quite adventurous to move to the more vociferous end of the ground and we felt quite grown up once we didn't have to stand with our parents.'

Although reliable Reg Pickett continued to skipper the side throughout 1959-60, a new figure of authority emerged in the form of big Andy Nelson, who Ramsey plucked from West Ham reserves and who proved to be a towering influence at centre-half. Off the field, Nelson was not averse to mucking in with the best of them, and colleague Len Garrett recalled with amusement the days when Nelson could be found wheeling a barrow to help the construction team working on the North Stand redevelopment.

On the occasion of Nelson's debut, the referee initially found himself without any linesmen, due to their late arrival, and an appeal went over the tannoy for two volunteers to step into the breach. The genuine linesmen eventually arrived shortly after kick-off.

In the first month of the new year, Ipswich pinned high hopes on a new arrival, Welshman Aled Owen from Bangor City. For the rest of the season, Owen, who had only learned to speak English at the age of fourteen, occupied the 'problem position' of right-winger as Town cruised to a respectable finishing position of eleventh.

By now, construction of Portman Road's first floodlights had been completed at a cost of £15,000, funded by the supporters' association. The lights were officially switched on by Lady Blanche Cobbold, as 16,000 curious spectators turned out for a friendly with Arsenal. The four pylons towered to a height of 110 feet and gave the ground a smarter and more professional look as the new decade got under way.

Larry Carberry leapfrogs over John Compton in this posed training photograph

Alf Ramsey in his not-so-plush office at Portman Road

Ken Malcolm (left) and Jimmy Leadbetter pose for this photograph on the practice pitch

Chapter Three

~ *Mounting a Challenge* ~

July-October 1960

After three unremarkable seasons consolidating in Division Two, during which time attendances had even started to slide, there was considerable onus on Alf Ramsey in the summer of 1960 to pull a few rabbits out of hats to revive interest in the club. An impartial observer might have considered that Ipswich Town was already 'punching above its weight' in Division Two, but Suffolk folk are a demanding lot and clearly wanted more than just mid-table mediocrity.

The forthcoming 1960-61 campaign represented the club's silver jubilee season – it had turned professional 25 years earlier – and although huge strides had been taken in that time, some of the enthusiasm generated in the town by the 1957 Third Division title win had begun to fade. Ramsey's response was to complete a batch of close-season signings that created little fuss at the time, but would ultimately have a huge impact on the club's fortunes. He also appointed a new skipper from within, when wing-half Reg Pickett asked to be relieved of the burden of that role. The new man tossing the coin and rallying the troops would be big Andy Nelson, who'd enjoyed a fine first season at centre-half, clearly thriving on first-team football after years on the fringes at West Ham, where he'd understudied Ken Brown.

Ramsey spent £6,400 on his four new men, which was relatively big bucks for Ipswich, but their names gave the fans little cause to get excited. Leicester were quite happy to offload little Roy Stephenson for £3,000. He was an inside-right or winger who'd failed to set Filbert Street alight in one season there. Goalkeeper Wilf Hall was surplus to requirements after managerial changes at Stoke City, and Town paid £2,000 to make him understudy to the popular Roy Bailey. Ramsey talked Chelsea into releasing inexperienced wing-half John Compton for a cut-price £1,000, and also signed a promising young defender called Bill Baxter from Scottish junior club Broxburn Athletic for £400. Baxter's strict father had insisted he finished an engineering apprenticeship before worrying about football, and his progress was also hampered by a forthcoming National Service call-up.

The right-wing position had given Ramsey a headache, ever since the departure of Billy Reed. Peter Berry had looked a decent replacement, but a serious knee injury in a 1959 reserve game cut short his career. Berry would later go into business with brother Johnny, the Manchester United player whose own career was ended by injuries in the Munich air crash. As Berry worked in vain to make a comeback, a series of replacements were tried in the No 7 shirt but none really looked the part. Ramsey had high hopes that Stephenson could be the answer and on meeting the player in London told him he was 'the final piece in the jigsaw'.

This was music to the ears of a man whose career was at a crossroads. Having just turned 28, Stephenson had been unable to hold down a regular first-team place at Blackburn and then Leicester. In later years he admitted he'd been close to returning to his native north but was won over by Ramsey, who used his quiet powers of persuasion to great effect in the noisy surroundings of Liverpool Street station. Nicknamed Rocky, Stephenson could be quick off the mark, tricky in possession and was a good crosser of the ball. Short and stocky, he was a qualified mining engineer and also a useful cricketer, having played in the Lancashire League. The move to Ipswich represented a last chance for his faltering football career. Reflecting in his later years, Stephenson would recall: 'Alf's attention to detail was amazing. In his Friday team talks he concentrated on trying to find weaknesses in the opposition. There were no long dossiers, he had all the information in his head. He had an incredible memory.'

By mid-September Stephenson had settled into his new surroundings and was providing a superb service to front-men Crawford and Phillips, prompting the *East Anglian Daily Times'* Tony Garnett to call his crossing 'as accurate as anybody in the game'. Compton and Baxter would have to wait longer to make an impact, the latter packing his bags to join the Royal Engineers at Aldershot. He was usually able to get time off for matches, but was not present for training in the week. Reserve players Rex Bryanton and Dennis Thrower were also called up to serve their country, but by the end of 1960 compulsory National Service was discontinued, to the relief of football clubs everywhere.

Goalkeeper Hall got an early chance to show his worth after Bailey was injured in a dreadful 0-4 hammering at Scunthorpe. Hall was given a big ovation from the Churchman's end on his debut against Derby, but it was his opposite number, Ken Oxford, who made all the headlines. Attempting to keep out a swirling cross from Aled Owen, Oxford crashed into a goalpost and suffered serious facial injuries. He was stretchered off unconscious and inevitably changed the course of the game which Town went on to win 4-1. 'WB of Ipswich' wrote a letter to the *Football Star* to say that although he didn't want to see subs introduced into football, it was unfair on Derby to lose their keeper in such circumstances. He called for a new law to force the other team to withdraw their own keeper when such an incident occurred, thus making things equal again. For good measure 'WB' also called for Town's players to save their congratulations till after the game in future – when the defence could join in if necessary – and thus stop the 'irritating back-slapping, handshaking, embracing and general cavorting' after a goal was scored.

This appeal for Town players to conduct their love-ins in private was made the same week as a summons on Penguin Books, alleging that D H Lawrence's novel *Lady Chatterley's Lover* was obscene. Predictably, this puritanical outburst led to the book's first print run of 200,000 selling out on its first day of publication. Two days after the Penguin controversy flared, certain Town players were accused of distasteful behaviour in a hard-fought home win over Liverpool. Ted Phillips juggled the ball and whacked home a brilliant goal but then the game degenerated into a series of niggly fouls and scuffles. An Ipswich fan wrote to the *Football Star* accusing Town of being out to 'needle' volatile Liverpool centre-forward Dave Hickson. 'Fair Play of Hasketon' agreed, adding: 'Extremely disgraceful tactics upset Hickson. I would have been grateful if a Town player had been sent off for the terrible display of baiting Hickson and another sent off for punching Hickson behind the ref's back – even if this did amuse large sections of the Ipswich crowd.'

The paper's editorial warned: 'If Ipswich are not very careful they will lose their reputation for good, clean football. Last season they and Plymouth were the only two clubs not reported to the FA for misdemeanours. But in the opening weeks of this campaign their reputation has slumped more than a little.' The local paper's letters column regularly proved that some Town fans demanded high standards. The occasional outbreak of barracking from the terraces – inside-forward

Doug Millward was often an unfortunate victim – underlined how they could be hard to please. Reporter Tony Garnett chided the boo-boys: 'The jeers only serve to make the players and spectators sour with one another. With full backing we might see a promotion-winning side,' he suggested.

Running the Town 'A' team at this time was former Manchester United and Northern Ireland international Harry Baird. Team member Mick Banthorpe recalls that Harry was a lively character who loved to sink a few pints after a game. He recalls: 'Our home games were played at Foxhall Stadium and on the team bus back into town after matches, Harry would suddenly lay low in his seat and issue instructions. If his wife was waiting on the corner of Wellesley Road we were to stop the bus for him to get off. If not, we could keep going and he would get his night out!'

The players certainly enjoyed a few laughs, but what was life like on the terraces in those days? Were the fans poorly served? According to one supporter, Jim Crane: 'You could get a pie or pasty behind the Churchman's Stand and there were toilets, but to be quite honest it was all a bit shabby in those days.' Fellow fan John Eastwood says: 'Peters Ice Cream had a tea bar and two or three huts around the ground. Girls also went round with refreshments on sale on a tray, rather like cinema usherettes. You could also buy hot Bovril, and I'm sure I'm not the only person who has only ever sampled this drink while at a football match.'

Eastwood recalls the main merchandise of the day being the tiny pocket-sized match programme (cover price 4d) and rosettes, while some fans had wooden rattles. Pre-match entertainment involved 'Swede' Herring walking around the perimeter of the pitch dressed in bowler hat and blue and white paraphernalia, attempting to rouse people into singing. According to John, this bus conductor from the Chantry estate was not an official mascot, but the club tolerated him and he became part of the scenery for many years. Sometimes he would be accompanied by a young lady dressed as a witch ('Miss Switch') and a schoolboy, Ian Harvey, in football kit.

Away from the ground, fans could buy an Ipswich Town necktie for 12s 6d, or 18s 11d for the luxury version, from Coe's department store in Norwich Road, which also sold blazer badges and mufflers. Fans who popped to the town centre Co-op store could admire 'lightweight, streamlined and flexible' Stanley Matthews football boots, newly on sale at £2 1s 6d in men's sizes.

On the pitch, new flanker Stephenson was introduced to the fans before the home game with Brighton, and helped inspire a 4-0 Town win that put them top of the table. It was not an entirely happy camp, however. Ted Phillips submitted a written transfer request, saying he was being starved of the ball and that he hankered for the sort of service he once got from now-retired Tom Garneys. He said he was also fed up commuting the eighteen miles by rail from his Colchester home. Phillips had in the past made verbal requests for a move, and his latest outburst had management and local press sighing with frustration. The *Football Star* called it foolish and hot-headed. A few days later, Phillips seemed to cheer up after hitting the target in a 5-2 away win at Leeds, and duly withdrew his request.

Phillips' antics often gave Ramsey cause for concern and the player himself recalled a training escapade from this period. He and skipper Andy Nelson were bringing up the rear on a road run, when they decided to hitch a lift from a passing sugar beet lorry. They were dropped off at a bus stop and caught a ride back to Portman Road, the conductor having recognised them and allowed them a free trip. They were soaking in the bath, feeling pleased with themselves, when a message came through that they were to report to Ramsey's office. The manager quietly asked if they normally hitched rides on lorries during training. Suitably chastened, the pair were ordered back to the ground in the afternoon for extra training. As it was a Thursday, lunch was at the Footman's store in town. While eating, rain begin to hammer down and the players were sure Ramsey wouldn't bother with extra training in such conditions. But after returning to the ground, they found the manager tracksuited and ready for them. Ignoring the dreadful conditions, Ramsey put himself in goal and ordered shooting practice to begin. After Phillips thrashed a few of his trademark thunderbolts at the drenched goalkeeper, Ramsey quickly called a halt to proceedings!

With or without the unsettled Phillips, Ramsey knew he needed reinforcements in the forward line. In early October he thought he'd got his man when tiny 32-year-old Spurs inside-forward Tommy Harmer agreed to come to Suffolk. A £6,000 fee was agreed but no fewer than 29 other clubs showed an interest and Ramsey was worried he might be outbid. Arranging over the phone to meet Harmer, Ramsey told him: 'In the meantime, I don't want to read in the papers that you've gone somewhere else.' Harmer reassured him, but that is exactly what happened and he chose to join Watford. Ramsey would have been willing to let Harmer live and train in London and was furious at being let down. Spurs came out of the episode well, however, for they pegged the fee at £6,000 when the huge interest could have resulted in a highly profitable auction.

Despite lacking strength in depth, the side maintained a consistent challenge near the top of the table throughout the autumn and confidence was sky high after the win at Leeds. With the home crowd depleted by a rugby international at nearby Headingley, the Elland Road side had schemer Don Revie in fine form and led 2-1 at the interval. But the tables were turned in dramatic fashion and Town knocked in four to dish out Leeds' worst home defeat since the war.

Town's League form deserted them in the brand new Football League Cup, in which Third Division Barnsley sneaked a 2-0 win at Portman Road, thus scoring the first opposition goals under the new floodlights. Ramsey took issue with those who condemned this new competition as an unnecessary distraction from the serious business of League football. The lethargic display against Barnsley had to be quickly forgotten, for a few days later the Tykes' neighbours Sheffield United came to town as League leaders. An awful error by normally reliable Kenny Malcolm gifted the Blades a winner and Town fans were grumbling again. It was a dull anti-climax of a game and the farmers among the crowd must have wished they'd stayed at home to concentrate on the new campaign to drive the coypu, a destructive South American rodent, out of East Anglia's fields.

Town's home form was distinctly uninspiring, and many fans will have cast envious eyes at Charlton, who were entertaining their customers with remarkable goal bonanzas. Following a 7-4 win over Portsmouth, the Valiants forced a 6-6 draw with Middlesbrough. The goals did flow for Town away from Suffolk, however. A thrilling 4-2 victory at Stoke followed the pattern of the Leeds win, with all Town's goals coming after they'd fallen two goals behind. But it was followed by another miserable home display, bottom-of-the-table Swansea winning 3-0 in the mud. It was a wretched way for Bailey and Elsworthy to mark their, respectively, 200th and 300th first-team appearances.

The remarkable contrast between home and away results was mystifying, with Ramsey suggesting that visitors raised their game at Portman Road because of the superb pitch and Town's high League position. Another idea mooted was that because Town always trained on their practice pitch next door, the players were not familiar enough with the main pitch.

Despite four home games without a win, Town clung to second place in the table, but had to suffer dwindling home gates. The 12,309 for the Derby fixture was the lowest for a season's opening home game since 1946. Only the turnout for the top-of-the-table clash with Sheffield United pleased the management. F Kistner of Ipswich wrote to the *Football Star* with his explanation: 'Crowds are disappearing for one simple reason – there are not the great players of the past to thrill and hold the public. Another factor is increased prices. Sir Stanley Rous and Alf Ramsey will argue that football at three shillings is still the cheapest form of entertainment. But Ipswich draw a big percentage of gates from outlying villages and these people have to make a round trip of something like 40 miles, so it doesn't stop at three shillings. I have also never been told before "your season ticket is now ready, come and get it". The club should have sent it to us by post as soon as we paid the lolly.'

When the supporters' club (ITSA) officially opened its new coffee bar and grill, even the guest of honour, the Mayor of Ipswich P J Fowler, joined in the debate about the disappointing attendances. He ticked off the thousands of fans who were being catered for by ITSA and its facilities, who ought to be attending games, but were failing to do so. Fan Paul Preston wrote to *Soccer Star* magazine to register 'disgust' at the fans for not turning out now that promotion might be on the cards. He said the same people had a few years earlier moaned that Third Division status wasn't good enough. Another follower, Bernard Blowers of Dunstable, attempted to be constructive, suggesting the club mount a publicity campaign whereby 'high pressure salesmen' would tour Ipswich and the surrounding countryside to mix with potential supporters in the pubs and clubs.

With more and more people now having their homes connected to the telephone network, it was becoming common practice to phone the football ground, or the local paper, to enquire about the latest score on matchdays. John Gardiner of ITSA had to issue a polite appeal for people to stop doing this, as he and fellow officials had to keep getting up from their seats during a match to answer the con-stantly-trilling phone!

Ramsey, meanwhile, was not being distracted from developing his tactical system of withdrawn wing-men. Both flankers, Stephenson and Leadbetter, were settling comfortably into their roles and proving to be key figures. The former was serving up pinpoint crosses from deep for the head of Crawford, and the latter's trademark was prob-ing passes into space for the marauding Phillips. The pair were dis-tinctly different in style and appearance, but had in common the fact that Ramsey had rescued their floundering careers.

Indeed, many observers found it hard to believe that the willowy figure of Leadbetter was thriving in Division Two at the age of 32, considering the stop-start nature of his career in his twenties. Pat Godbold, the manager's secretary, recalls that Leadbetter was fondly nicknamed 'Sticks' because of his spindly frame and rather elderly looks. One national newspaper even labelled him 'Steptoe's dad', but she felt this was rather unkind.

Leadbetter would later reflect on his role in the side: 'I was pulled back collecting balls from the defence. The full-backs wouldn't come that far out of defence to mark me, so I had space to move in. As I went further forward I could draw the full-back out of position. That left a big gap on the left-hand side of the field and that was where Ted played. He needed space but if you could give him that and the ball, it was in the back of the net.' Team-mate John Elsworthy added: 'With me also around, the system bamboozled defences as we always had one spare man to receive the ball and that spare man had time to play and we managed to make the most of it. Alf later did precisely the same thing with the England team.' John Eastwood gives the view from the terraces: 'Ramsey's tactics just baffled the opposition and it took them ages to work out how to combat it. Most fans were not par-ticularly aware of the system really and would shout at Leadbetter to get on his wing, not realising his positioning was deliberate.'

ITSA official John Gardiner knew what was going on, though, and noted: 'The Ramsey formation is now being honed to perfection throughout the club and was viewed to perfection in the reserves' 4-0 win over Brighton.' Leadbetter worked tremendously hard and won praise from Ramsey for his tackling and commitment. His gaunt, balding features disguised a tough character who was rarely injured. He made his 100th consecutive appearance in the autumn of 1961 and at this point had missed only three of the previous 199 games. 'We have relied heavily on Leadbetter in recent seasons and he has been the link between defence and attack,' explained Ramsey.

Not all supporters were convinced about Leadbetter's contribution, however. 'Town fan' from Stowmarket wrote in: 'We need a faster and stronger winger than Leadbetter. If Ramsey doesn't strengthen here, and at inside-right, promotion will be missed and it will kill support for the future.' G Humphries of Newmarket had similar views: 'Leadbetter hasn't the speed these days to make quick incisive openings, is unable to show his full-back a clean pair of heels and has to push the ball inside to one of the other forwards.' Others were more appreciative, however: a pitch-side benefit collection, inviting fans to lob coins into a blanket, collected £102 17s 7d for the winger. This represented more than four weeks wages for a man whose family were now happily settled in a club-owned house in Alpe Street.

Leadbetter may not have looked like an athlete, but he grafted hard and didn't let the taunts of away fans worry him. He was inspired by the faith Ramsey showed in him and in later years paid fulsome tributes to the manager. His favourite Ramsey tale illustrates how the boss was more down-to-earth than the public realised. Leadbetter tells how, while waiting for a train at Liverpool Street station, Ramsey suddenly announced to a group of players that they would go for some jellied eels. He marched them down the road to Tubby Isaac's stall, which he clearly knew well from previous visits. Here the smartly-dressed manager demonstrated the fine art of eating this East End delicacy, sprinkling on the hot chilli vinegar with skill and enthusiasm. The eels went down well, but not half as well as Ramsey's gesture.

Trainer-coach Jimmy Forsyth with Wilf Hall (left), Ken Malcolm (right) and some Ipswich reserves

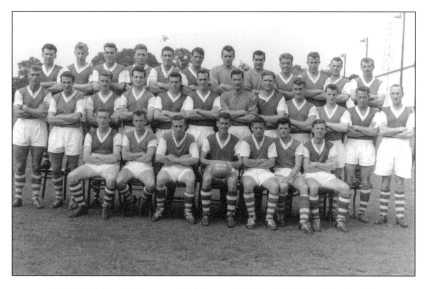

The 1960-61 Ipswich Town squad which won the Second Division Championship

This unusual photograph shows a gap for the missing Baxter. He would have been 'pasted in' later

This front cover of the Ipswich match programme was used throughout the championship season

Chapter Four

~ *Steadying the Ship* ~

November 1960 – February 1961

Town's perverse run of autumn form – winning away while losing at home – came to an abrupt end in November. Normal service resumed at Portman Road when Ray Crawford and Ted Phillips rediscovered their shooting boots for home games. The turning point was a somewhat disjointed contest, when bottom-of-the table Lincoln City were the visitors. The lowest home attendance in over four seasons of Second Division football was growing distinctly restless, until second-half goals finally sank Bill Anderson's lowly Imps. It settled the nerves and ended the home hoodoo.

Unfortunately this return to home form coincided with a run of defeats on the road and Ramsey stepped up his search for a new inside-forward. The supporters' association agreed to be guarantors for a £15,000 loan to the football club to finance some new blood and Ramsey missed the defeat at Sunderland to go window-shopping north of the border. Attracting players to unfashionable Ipswich was no easy task, but one carrot that Ramsey could dangle before potential recruits was a club house for the player and his family. His secretary Pat Godbold recalls: 'Around this time the club owned seventeen houses around the town. These could be an incentive for new players to come to Ipswich. The rent was only around £1 10s a week. Alf himself lived in a club house in Crofton Road for many years.'

A precious point was dropped in a thriller at Luton when Gordon Turner netted a last-gasp Hatters' winner and soon afterwards teenage sensation Billy McPheat destroyed Town at Sunderland with two spectacular goals. At Kenilworth Road, Town had been frustrated by keeper Jim Standen, making his home debut in place of fractured-skull victim Ron Baynham. Standen was a true all-rounder, for in the summer months he was a pace bowler with Worcestershire. Town's Phillips and Elsworthy were also useful cricketers, the latter having turned down the chance to sign for Glamorgan early in his career. Another star of both sports was Yorkshire and England batsman Brian Close, who played and scored against Town for Bradford City a few years earlier.

Across the Atlantic, a new era dawned in November 1960, when John Kennedy won the race for the White House against Republican rival Richard Nixon. JFK and his glamorous wife Jackie brought to an end an era of American stagnation, and radical change was in the air in the UK, too. The 1960s were under way and it was out with the old and in with the new. National Service call-ups were scrapped, a jury ruled that *Lady Chatterley's Lover* was artistic and not obscene, and betting shops were legalised. Working-class realism even took over London's West End, where the lives of East Anglian farmworkers came under the spotlight in Arnold Wesker's play *Roots*. Footballers wanted to be part of the revolution, too. They decided the maximum wage rule was a nonsense and they threatened strike action in a bid to be shot of it.

Ipswich Town's shop steward in the big pay row was inside-forward Doug Millward, who supported his union's stance but admitted he and his team-mates were keen not to lose the goodwill of the fans and see gates dwindle yet further. In common with most clubs, the entire Town squad were paid-up members of the Professional Footballers' Association (PFA) and were fully behind the strike call, although naturally anxious about the consequences of such a step. Millward confessed: 'You can imagine how I feel about this strike business. Ipswich saved me from going out of the League. They granted me a benefit and now in the first team I get top money. I owe everything to Ipswich and am grateful.'

For several weeks both sides in the dispute dug their heels in and all-out strike action looked increasingly likely. Millward, along with colleagues Andy Nelson and Roy Bailey, went to see Alan Everitt, sports editor of the *EADT*, to ask for his help in finding all the players work once the strike started. Only two of the squad had skills – Bailey as a painter-decorator and Nelson as a marine engineer – which meant the others would all be looking for labouring jobs. 'It's jobs we want, not sympathy,' emphasised Millward.

Town's entire wage bill was £700 per week at that time, although a ceiling of £20 existed on an individual's weekly pay packet. Pat Godbold recalled that she and Alf Ramsey would often travel into town to the bank to fetch the players' wages, which would be handed over in small brown envelopes: 'Over that period Alf was secretary-manager, although he didn't have to do all the administrative work.

Wally Gray was financial secretary and we all chipped in really. I would answer the phones, sell tickets and deal with enquiries and also do Alf's letters.'

The PFA wanted the maximum wage scrapped and for their members to have the freedom to negotiate their own deals with their club manager in future. This filled Alan Everitt with horror: 'It may sound absurd, but what is to prevent a player demanding to be replaced by his solicitor in his negotiations?' he wrote. His veiled prediction that 'agents' would end up doing the negotiating would prove absolutely spot on, of course, but it would take another 30 years or so for it to become a widespread reality.

Leading lights in the PFA's struggle were Cliff Lloyd and 32-year-old Jimmy Hill, who was in his last season as a player. The pair worked tirelessly to get the clubs to relent after they had initially refused to raise the wage ceiling from the maximum £20. Their eventual success set in motion the abolition of the entire system. This would lead to the players taking the revolution a step further when the old retain-and-transfer system, which the clubs saw as a cornerstone of the professional game, was successfully challenged in the High Court. Justice Wilberforce ruled that the system was an unreasonable restraint of trade, but strangely enough it would be many years before the players took advantage of his ruling and began to move freely at the end of their contracts.

As the proposed strike date of 20 January loomed, Town chairman John Cobbold went on Anglia TV to debate the issue with Jimmy Hill, but a day or two later the authorities caved in and the whole matter was resolved without industrial action. It was announced in early February that the maximum wage rule would be lifted in the summer and players would be free to negotiate their own pay deals. Hill's high profile during the dispute saw him quickly find media work after his club, Fulham, released him in 1961. He was offered the chance to be an ITV commentator at the FA Cup final, and although later returning to football as manager of Coventry City, the die was cast and he would go on to become a prominent media pundit for many years.

All parties seemed relieved that there would be no national strike, although there were worried faces in boardrooms across the country, for it was estimated that more than 60 percent of League clubs were in financial difficulties at this time. Ipswich Town, thanks to a frugal spending policy and its generous supporters' association, were not one of the worse off, but neither were they cash-rich. Town's PFA rep Millward was delighted the strike had been avoided, but had personal concerns over maintaining his own place in the side. With Ramsey still searching for a new inside-forward, Millward's future as a regular looked in jeopardy and his displays were the subject of much debate among fans. A stocky, dependable sort from solid northern stock, Millward was a talented tennis player who represented Suffolk during the summer. Although a wholehearted performer on the football field, he often seemed to attract barracking from sections of the crowd when things weren't going well for the team. Others, however, sang his praises and supporter Jack Warren of Ipswich wrote to the press: 'He's my type of player. He has speed, works hard together with team-mates and can stay the course for 90 minutes.'

Millward's finest hour had been when scoring a hat-trick against Leyton Orient in January 1960, a feat that was achieved against the same opposition a year later by Ray Crawford. Crawford's was a mar-vellous display by the centre-forward on a day when the lowest crowd for several years – under 10,000 – showed up at Portman Road to wit-ness a 6-2 hammering of Les Gore's side. With Christmas still a week away, the hat-trick took the lively Crawford up to the 23-goal mark, an average of more than a goal a game, and an Ipswich career total of 66 in 88 League games to that point. He was fast becoming a Portman Road legend, and the fans loved his energetic approach and willing-ness to chase anything and everything. Long-standing supporters' club official Tony Chittock, speaking 40 years later, had little doubt that Ray Crawford was the club's top player of all time, for the flamboyant way he played, his consistent scoring and his partnership with Ted Phillips.

A former office boy and building worker, Crawford was the son of a professional boxer. Having fallen out of favour with his local club Portsmouth, Ramsey snapped him up for £5,000 and he proved to be a shrewd signing. Nicknamed 'Jungle Boy' on the strength of his serv-ice with the Royal Hampshires in Malaya, he would modestly point out that he'd actually only ever done two patrols in the jungle and nothing untoward happened anyway. Slim and athletic, but deceptively strong in the air, Crawford played with a smile on his face and struck up a genuine rapport with the fans. His bubbly personality was loved at the club and Pat Godbold remembers him as someone who never stopped talking, a characteristic also true of one of his centre-forward successors, Paul Mariner.

Crawford's goals had made people sit up and notice and in the autumn of 1960 he received a call-up to play for an FA representative side against the RAF, alongside his less well known Ipswich team-mate, full-back Larry Carberry. With Ipswich in the Second Division, the two players and the club treated this as a great honour, but were dismayed when the match turned into an anticlimax, with most of the other players showing a distinct lack of enthusiasm for the occasion. The call-up was a boost for Carberry, a no-frills performer who was a reliable figure in the No 2 shirt and another excellent bargain capture by Ramsey. Short and solid in stature, Carberry wasn't outstandingly fast but distributed the ball well and was a full-back very much in the Ramsey mould. Carberry also used the ball simply and effectively, and made few mistakes.

Carberry would admit later he'd felt honoured by the manner in which Ramsey recruited him for Ipswich. He had been performing at non-league Bury Town while stationed with the army in West Suffolk. The story goes that Ramsey drove to Bury St Edmunds to watch him and was sufficiently impressed that he left his seat before the end of the game to walk around the ground and intercept the player as he came off the pitch. Carberry recalled: 'A national paper claimed it was the first time Alf had ever been known to leave his seat before the end of a game. I felt quite honoured.' Ramsey made such an impression on Carberry, a scouser, that the player joined Ipswich in preference to his beloved Liverpool, who had also made enquiries about him. His decision was greeted with great surprise by family and friends on Merseyside, but it was one Carberry never regretted.

Christmas at Portman Road meant the players would get their little bonus from Ramsey – a £2 shopping voucher to spend at the Footman Pretty department store. John Elsworthy says that although the players appreciated the gesture, it was regarded with amusement, particularly when Roy Bailey parked outside the store to spend his voucher and promptly received a £2 parking ticket! The same town-centre store was the venue for the weekly club lunches on Thursdays. These events saw the club foot the bill after the team had tucked into something a little more nourishing than the tea and lardy cake they might otherwise get from Jim's Café near the ground. Elsworthy remembers some of the players would hurry their Footman's lunch in order to get to the nearby cinema, because you could see a film for a reduced price of one shilling if you got there before 1.30pm.

Sitting just a few points off the top of the table at Christmas 1960, Town tackled a yuletide double bill against local rivals Norwich. Fans jostling for tickets were dismayed when a ceiling of 25,000 was put on the home fixture, even though 26,700 had been deemed a safe level for a home game with Luton less than two years earlier. It was pointed out by one local journalist that a firm of architects who inspected the ground said it could hold 30,000, with each person having eighteen inches of terrace space. Nevertheless the limit remained at 25,000 and home fans had to be consoled by the decision not to allocate any of the tickets to Canaries fans. Town supporters were welcome at the more spacious Carrow Road for the first game, however, and one even had the cheek to display a huge banner announcing 'we will pluck the Canary of its feathers.'

Feathers were indeed plucked in abundance as Ipswich ended City's twelve-month unbeaten home run and cruised to a 3-0 win, even though the home side forced fifteen corners to just one for Town. The following day, City came to Portman Road for the return, made several team changes, and took an early lead. But once Town shifted into top gear there was only one winner and a joyously received 4-1 triumph saw them go top of the table. Amid the jubilation of this double derby triumph, even the cautious Ramsey permitted himself to use the word 'promotion' when speaking to the gentlemen of the press.

A highlight of that home fixture with Norwich was the performance of young Billy Baxter who was called up for his debut in place of injured Ken Malcolm. The young soldier, released after a week's square-bashing at Aldershot, was a revelation, showing composure and strength in all he did. Baxter was an instant hit and, thanks to the agreement of his commanding officer, was made available for all the remaining League games for the 1960-61 season. Ramsey was grateful for this, expressing delight with Baxter's emergence at a time when injury had struck down his regular right-half Reg Pickett. Strangely enough, the National Service commitment that caused Baxter's absence from Portman Road during weekdays was scrapped by the Government in the very week that he made his first-team debut. The batch of 2,049 young British men who reported for duty in December was the very last group to find themselves compulsorily serving their Queen and Country.

In the same week that the one-millionth Morris Minor came off the production lines, Town stalled badly and were forced off the FA Cup road thanks to a nightmare afternoon at The Dell. Fellow Second Division outfit Southampton roared into a 6-0 lead by half-time of the third-round tie. Everything the George O'Brien-inspired Saints tried seem to come off, but Town's defence looked fragile and several of the goals were real gifts, particularly the first, which was down to an Andy Nelson blunder. Some pride was restored in the second half and the score finished 7-1, which is still a record cup defeat for Ipswich.

Confidence was restored a week later when Bristol Rovers were beaten 3-2 in a vibrant match at Portman Road. A feature of the game was an astonishing miss by Rovers' centre-forward Alfie Biggs, who seemed to freeze and then stumble when faced with an open goal. His howler was neatly described by the *Evening Star* as a case of 'putters twitch', and it prevented Biggs completing a hat-trick. Town kept the momentum going a week later with a splendid display at promotion rivals Liverpool. Bill Shankly's men were held to a draw, with Ted Phillips netting a wonderful drive that impressed even the partisan Kop. Town's defence was outstanding that day, particularly keeper Bailey, who later recalled: 'I remember arriving at Liverpool's Lime Street station and Alf made us travel the rest of the way to the ground on a public bus. He paid for the fares himself and off we went to play in front of a big crowd at Anfield on the top of this double decker.'

With the promotion chase hotting up, the supporters' association called for innovations to help the home crowd get into the swing of things. Their spokesman 'JAG' suggested pre-match community singing, a word or two from the players over the tannoy before games, entertainment from a brass band, better parking facilities, a new fans' song and a separate supporters' club for female fans. Chairman John Cobbold couldn't promise instant action on these colourful ideas, but he did announce that plans were afoot to improve the stadium. This was met with a degree of criticism from fans who felt a bigger priority should be strengthening of the team.

The normally-lethal Ted Phillips showed in February that he was only human when he missed a penalty for the first time in his professional career – his first aberration in thirteen attempts. Rotherham's Jack Wren was the brave custodian who got in the way of Phillips' twelve-yard bombshell – and considering this would be Wren's only senior game in English football, it was quite an achievement to be able to pass on to his grandchildren. In the pre-Christmas period, Phillips had been overshadowed by partner Crawford's scoring achievements and was not having the season he'd hoped for. 'Too often he gets into a rut and does little more than go through the motions,' complained the *Football Star*. By February, however, enigmatic Ted was looking a bit brighter, despite his penalty miss. After a slick exchange of first-time passes with Crawford, he cracked in a sensational goal against Leeds, but in the very next game blotted his copybook by trying to burst the net with an easy chance against Charlton, only to see the ball fly horrendously off target. One national paper called the miss 'comic'.

Phillips could be quite a comedian off the field, recalls Ramsey's secretary Pat Godbold. He loved practical jokes and was always close to the action when mischief was being made. Whenever Ramsey sent the players out of the ground on a road run during training, it would inevitably lead to antics of some sort once they were out of sight. When jogging round their usual circuit, the group would soon reach Chevallier Street, where the steep hill of Valley Road loomed up ahead of them. Faced with such a horror, a refreshment stop would be called for. As the houses numbered 51 to 65 in Chevallier Street had no enclosed frontage, their doorsteps abutted the pavement being traversed by the thirsty footballers. As a consequence, any bottles of milk standing there usually proved simply too tempting and were quickly guzzled.

Pat Godbold pinpoints Phillips and reserve David Deacon as the two Town players with the biggest reputation for larking around. Phillips would brighten up the club's austere offices most mornings when he would stride in, put his feet up on the table, hand over some apples and oranges to his white-collar colleagues and start reading his paper. The recipients wouldn't dare ask where the fruit came from. Anecdotes abound about Phillips, who seemingly was the 'Gazza' of his day. Supporter Jim Crane recalls one episode that involved a prank in a hotel lobby on the morning of an away match. Phillips somehow managed to borrow a top hat and tails from somebody, put them on and strode ostentatiously to the front of the hotel where a taxi cab dutifully swept up to ferry him away. Once the journey got under way Phillips announced from the back of the cab that he was not really a true toff, but was Lord Ted of Portman Road, and he would be wearing Ipswich Town's No 10 shirt later that day!

Despite the players' penchant for hitching rides on lorries and nicking other people's milk on training runs, there was no shortage of serious commitment on the club's practice pitch. In one spirited session, Ramsey himself played a full and active part in a game and injured his knee quite badly. In the same session trainer Jimmy Forsyth was accidentally knocked unconscious. In those days, unless it involved road or park runs, training was always held on the practice pitch behind the West Stand. Years later Bobby Robson would give the players a change of scene by introducing sessions at HMS Ganges, a naval training centre beside the Orwell estuary at Shotley. Eventually, of course, the club would set up a new training centre away from the stadium in Bent Lane, on the north-eastern edge of town.

Ramsey spent as much time as possible with his players and liked to join in training. He was not afraid of getting muddied on the practice pitch, but continued to cut a smart and dignified figure elsewhere. By now, he was visiting the bespoke Ipswich tailor Peter Little to have his suits cut. Mr Little later recalled: 'I can remember one day arriving back at my business after lunch to find Alf Ramsey and another client waiting for fittings. I asked who was first and Alf said that, as he had finished his work for the day, the other gentlemen should go first.'

As February drew to a close, a happy and settled Town side could reflect on an unbeaten run of ten games in the League that saw them handily placed just one point behind leaders Sheffield United, and ahead of Liverpool. After an up-and-down autumn, the ship had been steadied and the promotion chase was very much on. Home attendances were creeping upwards again and with twelve games remaining, even the most fickle of fans was beginning to believe that top-flight football really was within reach.

Ken Malcolm, Andy Nelson, Roy Bailey, Ted Phillips (holding umbrella) and Roy Stephenson outside the team's Manchester hotel, prior to Ipswich's first ever top division game, at Bolton

Crawford heads goalwards during Ipswich's first top division game, 0-0 at Bolton (August 1961)

Elderly supporters at the Churchman's End prior to beating Burnley 6-2 (August 1961)

Spurs keeper Bill Brown fists clear with Jimmy Leadbetter lurking (October 1961)

A group of Ipswich fans behind the North Stand prepare for the trip to Spurs (March 1962)

Chapter Five

~ *Maintaining Pole Position* ~

March-May 1961

Ipswich Town's most dramatic and important victory of the 1960-61 campaign came on a tense and thrilling night in Sheffield in early March – but sadly there were precious few Town fans there to enjoy it. Bramall Lane was packed to the rafters on this chilly Tuesday night for the meeting of Division Two's top two sides. Johnny Harris's Blades had weeks earlier been six points clear at the top, but now their lead had all but disappeared. They looked guilty of taking their eye off the ball due to their marvellous run in the FA Cup.

Their meeting with Ipswich had to be put back three days owing to an FA Cup quarter-final date at St James' Park, the home of First Division giants Newcastle. A hat-trick by Billy Russell saw the Blades shock the Geordies 3-1, clinching a semi-final place for the first time since the war. This achievement alone ensured a huge crowd and vibrant atmosphere for Ipswich's visit to a ground that was basically a three-sided affair in those days, standing adjacent to the county cricket ground. The sound of 35,000 celebrating Yorkshiremen might have proved an intimidating experience for the East Anglian visitors but captain Nelson and his men were made of stern stuff. After all, they'd already proved they could handle big occasions, having held Liverpool in front of a baying Kop a few weeks earlier.

Ted Phillips settled any lingering Town nerves with an emphatic first-half finish and the 'team of the moment' suddenly looked vulnerable. Town took control and played the Blades off the park. Ray Crawford's courage and persistence produced a second goal. He was injured, colliding with a defender in the act of scoring, but the handful of Town fans present were in dreamland. Ron Simpson lifted the home crowd briefly with a marvellous solo effort, but Town refused to cave in and Crawford sealed the victory from close range. It meant Ipswich had replaced United at the top of the table and an ecstatic chairman Cobbold called the display his club's best ever.

This was the night Town finally became serious title contenders in the rest of the nation's eyes and the result hit football like an H-bomb, according to *EADT*'s Alan Everitt. Flight Sergeant Blackman, stationed at nearby RAF Lindholme, was one of the few Town fans able to get to the game: 'What a wonderful match. I shouted myself hoarse to let them know they had at least one supporter among the 35,000. I can't understand why this Ipswich team isn't supported better. When Norwich were at Bramall Lane there were approximately 6,000 of their fans, but I failed to pick out any other Suffolk voices.'

The issue of Town's shortage of support also occupied the mind of Alan Hoby of the *Sunday Express*: 'Everything about Ipswich is different. They have the most upper-crust board I know – a baron in Lord Cranworth, a baronet in Sir Charles Bunbury, an Old Etonian chairman in John Cobbold, who is also the Prime Minister's nephew, and an Old Harrovian in Major Terry. Yet there is a most definite knock in the Ipswich engine, and it is caused – of all people – by the choosy, hard-to-please citizens of Ipswich. Some strange, dehydrating chemistry seems to choke the enthusiasm of Suffolk crowds.'

John Jacobs, supporters' club secretary, told Hoby that the reason was the temperament of the average Suffolk man: 'They are reserved down here. They seldom let their hair down. It's not only football – they'll take a long time making their mind up about anything.' Cobbold had his own idiosyncratic take on the situation: 'When I last looked in the accounts we were just 9s 11d in the black. Another 5,000 at the gate would make all the difference between butter and marge.'

Although resources were limited, manager Ramsey continued his search for a new forward. This was not good news for Dubliner Dermot Curtis. He was down the pecking order, beneath Doug Millward and Derek Rees, who normally occupied the No 8 shirt, and Crawford and Phillips' were rock solid at 9 and 10. Curtis decided his best course of action would be to seek employment elsewhere. He asked for a transfer, but a week or two afterwards found himself in the team, and duly scored three goals in five matches. These left him on eighteen goals from 32 first-team games – but he was still far from being a regular. Ramsey had no such dilemmas concerning the men on defensive duties at this time. Skipper Andy Nelson was a tower of strength and hard-tackling newcomer Bill Baxter was showing unexpected maturity and consistency.

Baxter's displays hid a high-pressured lifestyle. He would rush to join his team-mates on Saturdays after a week's square-bashing with the Royal Engineers at Aldershot. In addition he was unable to spend much time with wife Dot and son William, who were hundreds of miles away in Scotland. Yet he took it all in his stride, completing his National Service in the knowledge that if his football dreams faded, he could fall back on an apprenticeship already completed in industry before signing for Ipswich. Broadcaster David Coleman was intrigued by Baxter's lifestyle and wrote of the debt the player owed to his father, an engine driver from Edinburgh: 'Baxter was told of his mistakes in downright Scottish fashion, and sent out training when he would have preferred to put his feet up by the fireside. Baxter senior would take his lad to the beach in bitter weather and despatch him into the sea to soak his bruises, even though the water was so cold the player thought it would kill him.'

Baxter recalled: 'One night my father locked me out for breaking training, and it was one in the morning before my mother could slip down and open the door to let me in.' Baxter had been totally focused on football from the age of nine, even during the engineering apprenticeship insisted upon by his father. Many years later, the player would recall how his generous sergeant major at Aldershot would permit him to disappear at weekends to play for Ipswich in 1960-61. For a spell, however, a new officer appeared on the scene who wasn't keen on sport and refused such concessions. A quick call by Baxter to a newspaper led to publicity about the situation and the new officer soon reconsidered. Despite all the inconvenience, Baxter felt his soldiering actually helped his football because it made him superfit. He would often play three major games a week – for the Army, his squadron and Ipswich – not to mention regular basketball during the week. He cut a trim and muscular figure, with ramrod straight posture, short back and sides haircut and thin-lipped, unsmiling face. He was four inches short of six feet, but very strong in the air. He reckoned the basketball helped him learn to time jumps and hang in the air, a technique he deliberately developed.

During the 1960s Baxter would establish himself as one of the most uncompromising defenders in English football. He benefited from playing during an era when bookings and sending-offs were relatively uncommon. Looking back he could only recall one booking in 459 games and reckoned that was when his victim dived. As well as dishing out bone-crunching tackles, Baxter could take punishment too, and it would need to be a pretty serious injury before he would leave the field. He recalled one incident at Aston Villa, where he was kicked in the face but played on, covered in blood and with 'bone sticking out of my head.' The Baxter fighting spirit was a key ingredient of the 1961 side and helped win crucial points, even when his colleagues were not performing to full potential. This was illustrated when Stoke came to town in March and refused to be intimidated by Ipswich's new status as League leaders. Galvanised by the recent arrival of manager Tony Waddington, Stoke looked like pinching a point but Baxter continued to drive Town forward deep into injury-time and the match eventually turned on a dramatic incident after 91 minutes' play. Referee Williams awarded a goal-kick, but then changed his mind and gave a corner to Town after a posse of players persuaded him to consult a linesman. Stoke were furious and still in disarray when the flag-kick came over. The ball was not cleared properly and bounced to John Elsworthy, who gently lobbed in an unlikely and rather lucky winner in this, Town's 200th Second Division game.

A week later Don Revie became player-manager of fellow Second Division outfit Leeds, who were slipping down the table and in need of fresh blood. Town did the double over the Yorkshiremen in 1960-61, scoring nine goals in the process, and not even Leeds' pop-singing winger Colin Grainger could hit the right note in two one-sided contests. Grainger, a full England cap, started his showbiz career after being persuaded to sing at an England post-match banquet. His impressive performance led to theatre engagements, TV appearances, recording contracts and a couple of minor chart hits. Grainger reckoned his glamorous double life wasn't making him rich, but it did help him purchase a smart Riley Pathfinder car. Even Chelsea starlet Jimmy Greaves could only afford a Ford Prefect at the time.

With second-placed Sheffield United contesting an FA Cup semi-final with Leicester, Town knew a win at Plymouth would put them three points clear at the top of Division Two. However, the build-up to the game was dominated by a dispute over where it would be played. Following hooliganism at Argyle's Home Park, the FA had got tough and closed the ground for fourteen days. It was agreed that Town's visit would be switched to Tottenham's White Hart Lane, but at the eleventh hour Plymouth's directors had a change of heart. They pressurised all parties into switching again, to Torquay's Plainmoor –

still neutral, but much nearer to home. Crucially, they were supported in their proposal by Town's promotion rivals Sheffield United and Liverpool, who (rightly) had felt it unfair for Town to be spared the long trip to Devon. Torquay may be a more attractive place than Tottenham, but at this late stage those Ipswich fans who had already bought tickets for White Hart Lane were furious. Happily, Crawford had the last word by scoring a late winner.

Ipswich then played host to Luton Town in another match for which the kick-off was switched. This time it was put back by four hours to avoid a clash with Grand National coverage on TV. Ipswich supporters had no problem with this change, and at last the club got the bumper attendance it had craved – nearly 22,000 packing Portman Road expecting to see Sam Bartram's erratic side beaten. Commencing a slide that would see them drop from Divisions One to Four in just five years, the Hatters nevertheless rose to the occasion and surprisingly inflicted Town's first home defeat since October, when Scots wing-half Alwyn McGuffie pounced on a rare Nelson error to fire the winner.

Six days later, Town made amends with a 3-1 Good Friday win over Middlesbrough. Encouragingly, the bumper Luton crowd was bettered by 500 and the terraces were so packed that youngsters were permitted to climb over the perimeter wall and sit on the grass to watch. It gave the wide-eyed lads the chance to get a close-up view of Boro's star centre-forward, the free-scoring Brian Clough. Crawford was not going to be overshadowed by Clough, however, and responded to the big match atmosphere in characteristic fashion, netting a couple of thrilling goals.

Dennis Thrower, a local product who had grafted away in the reserves for several seasons, was rewarded at this game for his long service with a benefit collection. This involved four people arranging themselves at each corner of a large blanket and walking slowly around the ground with the crowd invited to lob coins in their direction. John Bloom, then a teenage fan from Old Newton, recalls: 'These blanket collections would come round the pitch and people would have fun throwing the coins. Many would deliberately miss the blanket and it all got quite lively. In fact, in those days it was very common to see people in the crowd standing there with a crash helmet on. Maybe this was the reason.'

The blanket yielded £77 for Thrower, which was at least a month's wages at the time. The fans were more generous at a later game when the blanket was hoisted on behalf of goalkeeper Roy Bailey and £200 worth of coins were collected. Mascot Swede Herring would often assist the blanket operatives, and his burly figure inevitably took the impact from dozens of coins, a barrage he seemed to enjoy and which certainly amused the fans. Pat Godbold recalls that blanket collections were eventually stopped as the coin-throwing became rather dangerous. Years later, the likes of Bobby Robson, Kevin Beattie and Allan Hunter would enjoy testimonial occasions that would yield many thousands of pounds with never a blanket in sight.

Phillips conjured up a couple of Easter specials the day after the Middlesbrough game, when Town travelled to Huddersfield and chalked up a 3-1 win, achieved in no small part thanks to a series of great saves by Bailey. The promotion challenge wobbled a little on Easter Monday in the return at Middlesbrough. In what was another eventful game for Bailey, Brian Clough's close-range shot hit the keeper full in the face and knocked him cold. Bailey played on and was still dazed minutes later when the home side went ahead through a rare goal by Scot Ramon Yeoman. A Phillips 'special' levelled things, but Town collapsed to defeat in the dying minutes. The destination of the title was still unclear, but promotion had become tantalisingly close thanks to the four-point Easter haul.

Easter Monday was a big day for young Mick Banthorpe, a new face at Portman Road, who was given a debut in the reserves against Cardiff. Fresh from his National Service in the RAF, Banthorpe was hungry to break into the big time. 'I was told to report to the ground by 1.15pm for the Cardiff game, but we were all rather shocked when it was discovered there was nobody around to brew up the tea. Reg Pickett, the former first-team captain, immediately took charge of the situation and marched us all along to the Peters tea bar beneath the Churchman's Stand and here we got the important brew.' He recalled a crowd of around 3,000 for this routine reserve game, and says other fixtures attracted even more.

By the time Ipswich welcomed Freddie Cox's relegation-bound Portsmouth to Suffolk, promotion was tantalisingly close – just a point or two away, depending on results elsewhere. With the big prize within grasp, Town began showing signs of nerves, allowing lowly

Pompey to take the lead within 60 seconds of the kick-off. Phillips quickly levelled from the penalty spot and then transfer-listed Curtis marked his first appearance of the season with a fine header to put Town ahead. The lead lasted just minutes, however, and the rest of the game saw Town pressing nervously for a winner, looking vulnerable to counter-attacks. It wasn't what the fans expected of title-chasers, and the result left Ramsey's men just a point clear of Sheffield United and three ahead of Liverpool, with all three teams having four fixtures remaining. A rare treat for those Town fans possessing a TV was to see the goals shown that evening on BBC's Sports Special.

Given his usual caution and reticence with the media, Ramsey seemed happy to talk about promotion long before it was actually achieved. When asked about the suitability of big wing-half John Elsworthy for Division One football, instead of refusing to answer such a hypothetical question, he sprang to the Welshman's defence, saying Elsworthy would adapt well to the top flight, although he might need to introduce a greater sense of urgency to his game.

After struggling at home to Portsmouth, Town's next challenge was at Sincil Bank, home of another relegation candidate, Lincoln City. Seven coach-loads of fans trundled up the A45 towards the Fens, accompanied by a fleet of private and privately-hired vehicles, in addition to the hundreds going by rail. Again Town made a shaky start and within twenty minutes the huge away following was silenced by a Lincoln goal. It took a highly controversial sequence of events to settle nerves. Moments before the interval, Jimmy Leadbetter forced the ball in but referee Bullough ruled it out, having initially signalled a goal. The official was in the spotlight again five minutes after the break, when Town again bundled the ball into the City net. He disallowed this effort for pushing, but within seconds again caved in and changed his decision after vehement protests from Town players. The massed away fans behind the goal didn't know whether to laugh or cry. This equaliser was later agreed by the players to have been scored by Crawford, but remains in most record books in Phillips' name. Whoever actually scored, it certainly opened the floodgates. Three more strikes against a flimsy defence made the points secure and the table afterwards showed that promotion was by now virtually certain. Only a mathematical improbability could prevent it. One point from the last three games would be enough.

Anglia TV clearly didn't believe that fate could intervene. Without waiting for that final point to be won, they presented the club with a trophy to mark the first occasion a side from East Anglia had reached Division One. Two days later, in a party atmosphere at Portman Road, Town coolly and methodically destroyed Sunderland. Alan Brown's talented young team was without its most experienced performers – Charlie Hurley and Harry Hooper, both injured – and the youngsters were brushed aside. A crowd of over 21,000 – many of whom arrived hours before the kick-off – roared its delight as Town went ahead early with a soft goal. Keeper Pete Wakeham, distracted by the inrushing Curtis, misjudged a tame header from Elsworthy and the ball cleared his huge peaked cap and drifted into the net. Crawford headed a second to get the party in full swing. Ramsey himself appealed over the tannoy at half-time for people to keep off the pitch at the end. He must have been joking.

The roar that greeted Curtis's spectacular third goal was so loud that, according to the *Football Star*, it would have disturbed the rooks in Christchurch Park on the other side of town. A memorable 90 minutes was rounded off when Phillips was brought down by the keeper and a defender handled the loose ball, thus giving referee Fussey two reasons to award a penalty. Ramsey's earlier request was duly ignored at the final whistle and hundreds of youngsters followed Nelson and his team around the pitch on a joyous lap of honour.

Promotion was celebrated by Town personnel in their own particular ways. Chairman Cobbold cracked open the champagne, but his manager took a more sober approach. Cobbold would later enjoy telling the tale of how, an hour or so after the match ended, he found Ramsey sitting alone in the stands watching the Shaw Cup final between Ipswich and Norwich schoolboys, which kicked off shortly after the main game ended. When it was all over, encouraged by his ebullient chairman, Ramsey allegedly handed over his coat, climbed over the perimeter wall and with no one else watching did a one-man lap of honour!

It was a remarkable feat to have risen from the Southern League to the top flight in just 23 years, five of which were inactive due to the war. Leslie Page of the *Soccer Star* reflected on the romantic rise of the little guys: 'Just off the A12 at the entrance to Ipswich stands a sign which says Football Traffic This Way. Get, if you can, a man on a motorcycle to lead you through the narrow winding streets of this market town, as I did, and suddenly you arrive at Portman Road. Young ladies selling programmes, a crowded pressbox swollen by 'Lunnon' journalists anxious to discover how a club that only became professional 25 years ago are at the point of no return, with the rich cream of upper class soccer stretched before them. There are many who wonder how Ipswich will fare in faster company. They might be an in-between team unless the club is prepared to import a few players. With the material available, Mr Ramsey has triumphed against the odds.'

Just three hours after the conclusion of the Sunderland game, the Woodbridge Excelsior band struck up and a motley procession moved off from Portman Road heading for the town centre. Behind the band was an open-topped Land Rover bearing the standing figures of Ramsey, Cobbold and skipper Nelson, each wearing raincoats due to the weather, followed by three coaches containing players, wives and officials and a few specially-selected loyal fans. The vehicles slowly processed via Princes Street, Museum Street, High Street, Crown Street, Majors Corner, Carr Street and Tavern Street to the Cornhill, amid swelling crowds all the way. Mick Banthorpe recalls: 'As an "A" team player I was part of the parade, sitting on the roof of a coach with the sunroof pulled back. We had a laugh because the coaches actually left Portman Road in the wrong order. Leading the way was the Land Rover with John Cobbold, and then came us "A" team lads, followed by the first team. We milked the applause, but the order got changed after Ray Crawford noticed what was going on and put us in our place.'

At the Town Hall the party was greeted by the Mayor, P J Fowler, who announced: 'This fine town of ours, the first in East Anglia to attain championship football, will now be even more widely known throughout the British Isles.' The crowd assembled on the damp Cornhill cheered everything that moved, even a public service bus that accidentally got caught up in the melee when innocently trying to head for the village of Iken. The fans had been waiting impatiently since shortly after 5pm and were reluctant to respond to efforts to get them to sing Abide With Me. The anthem Why are We Waiting? was instead given several lusty renderings until the conquering heroes finally appeared after 8pm. With all this fuss going on in the town centre, opportunist thieves broke into the wooden offices at Portman Road, no doubt hoping to locate the £3,000 takings from the Sunderland gate. They broke open the safe, but found the office staff had diligently followed usual procedures and the gate money was nowhere to be seen. All they could grab was £5 from bike park receipts and, of this meagre haul, the coppers were dumped on the practice pitch, leaving the thieves with around £3 in silver coins for their trouble.

On the Monday evening, Town headed up to Derby's Baseball Ground, knowing a single point would see the Second Division Championship clinched. After a real struggle for 81 minutes, they blasted three goals in the final nine minutes and the silverware was in the bag. FA secretary Stanley Rous, among many to send messages of congratulation, mentioned how proud the late Captain Ivan Cobbold would have been to see this day. Back in Ipswich a local jeweller sought permission from the football authorities to present wristwatches to each player to mark their achievement. The title celebrations got under way in the same week the Government applied to join the Common Market. Curiously, Ipswich Town – exactly one year later – would 'get into Europe' before the nation did.

The final game of the season – at Swansea – became rather meaningless, and saw the home side win 2-1 with a last-minute goal. The Swans' players had formed a guard of honour to applaud Town onto the pitch and for Ramsey it was a proud afternoon, despite the scoreline. Ipswich's goal completed 100 for the season and was another long-range effort by Phillips. His manager commented: 'It was a fantastic shot and could not have been more fitting to complete the century of goals. It was going so hard the goalkeeper made no attempt at a save. I doubt if I shall ever see another goal quite like it.'

The Second Division trophy was presented three days after the season ended at a testimonial game for winger Peter Berry, whose career had been ended by injury. After an entertaining 3-3 draw with West Ham, watched by 10,524, Len Shipman of the League's management committee made the presentations and added: 'On your exhibition tonight I am sure you will hold your place in Division One next season.' One man who didn't pick up his medal that night was John Elsworthy, who'd departed on holiday to his native Wales.

Among those invited to the championship banquet a week later was former manager Scott Duncan and also Bill Baxter's commanding officer. The players received a 'talent money' bonus from the club, which amounted to £1,100 being shared among nineteen players, according to how many games they played. The lifting of the maximum wage, effective from that summer, meant wages were a big talking point and Town players wondered how they would fare in any forthcoming negotiations, now that they were among the elite. Players in the English game had till now earned no more than £20 a week, meaning envious eyes were cast towards Scotland, where Glasgow Rangers paid their men £25 a week, plus bonuses.

Ramsey announced that of his 34 professional players, 27 would be retained. Basil Acres and Peter Berry were retiring and five young hopefuls were released on 'frees'. Among the five whose career dreams were shattered at this point was local lad Russell Pelling. It meant an end to Pelling's regular routine of racing home from training on his bike to meet his girlfriend who worked in Boots, so they could ride home together at lunchtime. The girl in question, now Elizabeth Montgomery of Hampshire, remembers how 'Russell used to finish training at Portman Road and would ride his racing cycle up to Barrack Corner and wait for me to come along from Boots on my own racing cycle. These machines were the "in" mode of transport at the time. This would be at 12 noon and we would cycle home together as we both lived at the top end of Bramford Lane. On Sundays we sometimes went to the Ritz Cinema in the Buttermarket on the No 8 bus and most people would recognise Russell and say hello to him. We used to go dancing at the Manor Ballroom, which is where most of the footballers used to go. During the week, before or after training, some of them would go to Lyons tea rooms, along from the Cornhill.'

Ipswich Town's exploits were not the only reason Suffolk made national headlines that week in May. A 20-year-old local woman, Toni Gardiner, became engaged to marry King Hussein of Jordan and would from now be known as Muna Al Hussein (Hussein's choice). Strange times indeed.

St John Ambulance men and an expectant crowd at the Churchman's End

The eleven regulars who won the League title. None made fewer than 37 appearances in 1961-62

Roy Stephenson leaps for a cross in the vital home match against Aston Villa (April 1962)

Aston Villa goalkeeper Nigel Sims dives at the feet of Ray Crawford (April 1962)

Ted Phillips (cente) sends a thunderbolt shot wide of the Aston Villa goal (April 1962)

Ray Crawford stretches to keep the ball in play against Aston Villa (April 1962)

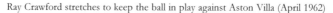

Chapter Six

~ *The Big Adventure* ~
July-October 1961

Hardly had the cheers died down from the promotion success than work began on improving and enlarging the North Stand end of the ground in readiness for bigger crowds in Division One. The workmen had to be on their best behaviour during July when the Queen passed by during a visit to the town. The ground capacity was raised to 29,000, but the stadium still retained a 'lower division charm' – which is perhaps a polite way of saying it was the most humble and sparsely appointed venue in 1961-62's First Division. The directors shelved plans to build new offices and dressing rooms in favour of the North Stand project. The funds for this came largely from the supporters' club, who regularly paid for ground improvements to allow the football club to concentrate on improving the team. It was common practice in 1961 for supporters' clubs to prop up their football club with cash injections. The money was needed all the more in view of a nationwide slump in attendances at the start of the 1960s.

A suggestion that Town's coffers be boosted by pitch-side advertising was pooh-poohed by chairman Cobbold: 'We don't think for a relatively small income it is worth having enormous coloured pictures all over the place,' he pronounced. Meanwhile, the players licked their lips at the prospect of fatter pay packets following the lifting of the maximum wage. Even so, some were still keen to take extra work over the summer to boost their earnings. Skipper Andy Nelson recalls that he and full-back Kenny Malcolm helped the workmen on the North Stand project. The sight of the Ipswich Town captain wheeling a barrow around in the hot sun became familiar to passers-by that summer.

A product of youth football in London's gritty docklands, Nelson had turned professional with West Ham in 1953, but National Service interrupted his progress and he found himself understudy to Ken Brown for long periods. After joining Ipswich at the age of 24 in 1959, Nelson went straight into the side and never looked back, cutting an imposing, rock-like figure in central defence. Tall and muscular, he loved physical battles with centre-forwards and built a reputation as a no-nonsense performer. He did his job and no one seemed concerned about his lack of speed or unwillingness to go forward. In fact, he would end his Ipswich career without scoring a single goal in over 200 games.

While his skipper was getting stuck in on the North Stand building site, manager Ramsey headed to Majorca for a well-earned two-week break with wife Vickie and daughter Tania. On his return he examined the new season's fixture list and shuddered. He told a supporters' club gathering: 'We have certainly got something on our plate and, sometimes, when I look at the places we have got to go, I am frightened and ask what I have done to deserve this? We have got to improve, but I am certain we shall. To those who say we shall go down as quickly as we came up, I say wait and see.'

Ramsey's words increased the sense of anticipation among Town fans and many could think of little else as the big kick-off drew nearer. But life continued in the outside world: among the stories making the headlines that summer was the suicide of author and adventurer Ernest Hemingway, the defection of ballet dancer Rudolf Nureyev, the wedding of the Duke of Kent and the creation of the Berlin Wall. Elsewhere in East Anglia, the future Princess of Wales, Lady Diana Spencer, was born.

Ramsey worked his men hard in pre-season training, with lots of road running. He would limit the long-distance runs once the season got under way, though, anxious not to tire his ageing squad, and introduced more ball work and five-a-side sessions. His philosophy was that he didn't need a team brimming with genius if there was a solid tactical foundation to build from with players of intelligence, willing to work and learn and possessing character. He kept training interesting with light-hearted games such as 'foot cricket', played with a tennis ball, and using feet instead of a bat. Ray Crawford recalled those training sessions: 'Wednesday was out on the road for ten miles with trainer Jimmy Forsyth and his peg leg, and while we were running Ted Phillips would disappear and go scrumping or something silly – Ted was the comedian. Alf worked on team play, wanting the ball to do the work. He wasn't keen on individuals, they didn't fit in with his plans.' Jimmy Leadbetter remembered: 'Alf loved being out among the boys on the training field. And he loved playing against me because he was faster than me.'

The national press issued dire warnings that Town would be in big trouble in the top flight if they didn't strengthen the team, but Ramsey knew exactly what he wanted. His only signing was inside-forward Doug Moran from Falkirk for £12,300. He'd monitored Moran for many months and had seen some of the 33 goals he notched in 1960-61 to help Falkirk win promotion. A small, fair-haired and athletic figure who answered to the nickname 'Dixie', Moran had an alert football brain, moved quickly when in possession and had a good eye for goal. He looked a good acquisition, but had a quiet start. He later recalled how his manager used to talk football non-stop on away trips. And when Moran first arrived from Scotland, practical joker Phillips ushered him into the train carriage occupied by Ramsey, while the other players sat as far away as possible. Someone had to listen to Ramsey, so it might as well be the new boy.

A week before the season started, Arsenal were held 3-3 in a Highbury friendly, giving cause for optimism about the tough battles ahead. The 'experts' were certain Town would find life difficult and one local bookmaker briefly offered 150-1 against Town ever topping the table during 1961-62. Another quoted them at 6-4 to be instantly relegated. The *EADT*'s Alan Everitt announced he had put £1 each way on Town winning the title at 100-1. Odds like these didn't worry shrewd Ramsey, who recalled that back in his days as a player the established sides usually paid little heed to newcomers, rarely spying on them or worrying about their tactics. He knew the big boys would be viewing Ipswich as mere cannon fodder. He felt this could be turned to his advantage.

Portman Road was now split into four distinct sections, meaning an end to some fans' habit of changing ends at half-time. Admission prices were set at 4 shillings (boys 2s) for the terracing, 3s (1s 6d) for uncovered standing in the Chicken Run, and 6s 6d for a seat. One national journalist appealed in vain for a better pressbox in the Chicken Run stand. 'To walk into it is hazardous – if you stand up straight you get biffed by a beam,' he complained. Creature comforts were certainly few and far between for the hacks. Even the local *Football Star* reporters had to suffer: Apprentice typesetter Graham Cook had to cycle to and from the paper's Carr Street offices to collect hand-written updates from reporter Tony Garnett in the cramped pressbox. Telephones? They were a luxury in this part of the world.

Town's first two fixtures in their debut season in Division One were both away in Lancashire, so Ramsey booked the team a five-day stay at the Queen's Hotel in Manchester. Although Manchester's reputation for wet weather is said to be exaggerated, the skies opened on the visiting party from Suffolk throughout all five days of their stay. The only compensation was being able to 'borrow' Manchester United's training facilities at The Cliff.

Town held their own in the opening game at Bolton, but chances were few and far between and the contest ended goalless. Nat Lofthouse, recently-retired Bolton and England centre-forward, conceded he might have been a bit hasty in writing off Ipswich's chances in the top division: 'They showed good teamwork and slick use of the ball – they're no duck eggs,' he said. The second task of Ipswich's Lancashire mission was to tackle multi-talented Burnley, champions in 1959-60, and a classy and innovative side. Star performer Jimmy McIlroy was now earning a reported £70 per week, more than four times the average British working man, and three times as much as most Town players. The Clarets had developed special tricks, such as secret signals before throw-ins and corners, so that team-mates knew what was coming. The game was a thrilling spectacle, with end-to-end attacking football throughout. Phillips gave a stunning performance in his 100th consecutive game, conjuring up four glorious long-range drives. The first, an early effort that stunned the crowd, hit a post, with keeper Adam Blacklaw rooted to the spot. Three times Burnley went ahead, but three times Town equalised. Sadly a defensive slip near the end saw it end 4-3 to the home side, but Ramsey called it the best Ipswich display he'd witnessed and John Elsworthy says it was the finest game he ever played in.

Town experienced teething problems at the first home game, with eager fans damaging two gates and climbing barriers before kick-off against Manchester City. Some supporters complained they were squeezed in so tight they 'couldn't even get a fag out of our pocket', while others were able to sit on the terracing during half-time with space to spare. Another First Division innovation – 7d for a cup of tea – didn't go down well either. Elvin King, then a teenage fan and later an *Evening Star* sports writer, remembers the excitement of the opening game: 'I stood in the new North Stand for the first time. None of us had thoughts of the title, we were just happy to be in the top flight.' The sense of anticipation began to evaporate when full-back Ken Malcolm was injured in the opening minutes. He subsequently missed the rest of the season with sciatica and one wonders whether his summer on the building site played a part in his back trouble. It proved a lively, rough-and-tumble game, with Town succumbing 2-4 to two late goals after looking potential winners for 80 minutes. Just one point from three games! Had the prophets of doom got it right? Were Town destined to be the eternal gallant losers?

Such negative thoughts were blown away in the fourth match of the campaign, the return with Burnley on a balmy Portman Road evening. Amazingly, the seven-goal thriller at Turf Moor was eclipsed by an eight-goal bonanza this time round. All five Town forwards got on the scoresheet – the first time this had happened since 1939. What a way to chalk up the first win. Four goals flew in during the first 22 minutes, the last of which was a header by new-boy Moran, which put Town 3-1 ahead and knocked the stuffing out of Burnley. Town never looked back from this point and fully deserved the plaudits for a wonderful 6-2 success.

Prior to kick-off, it had been a gloriously hot day, and north Suffolk-based supporter Mike Booth had been out in the fields harvesting since 5am: 'The game provided the sort of entertainment one can only dream of,' he wistfully remembers. Fellow supporter Steve Prentice recalls: 'It was a wonderful occasion, and was the moment we realised our unfashionable heroes could actually win a match in such hallowed company.' According to one press report, 'Town savaged highly rated Burnley and ripped searing gaps in their defence.' Noting that the Lancastrians had won the 1960 championship with basically the same side, this correspondent, with tongue firmly in cheek, suggested perhaps Ipswich would now do likewise.

It was certainly a red letter day for inexperienced John Compton, making his debut at full-back in place of Malcolm. The former Chelsea wing-half looked perfectly at home in his new role, apart from an occasional tendency to get rid of the ball slightly too hastily and in wayward fashion. This could be put down to nervousness and would soon vanish from his game. Dark-haired and determined looking, when a winger was tackled by Compton, he knew he'd been tackled. His debut delighted Ramsey, who had pondered the full-back situation even before Malcolm's injury. Compton had been tried at full-back in the opening reserve game of the season, and had done well. When Ramsey realised he would have to throw Compton in against Burnley's talented winger, John Connolly, he knew he would have to prepare his man beforehand. So, one afternoon after training, Ramsey summoned 17-year-old reserve winger Noel Kearney and told him to run full pelt at Compton with the ball, darting and feinting in Connolly fashion. According to Kearney, 'I ran at John like Alf said, and Alf taught John how he wanted him to play. It didn't work out too badly, did it?'

By the end of August, little Ipswich were halfway up the Division One table and had smashed eleven goals in their last three games. It was a great time to be a Town fan and Ramsey's blue and white army was spreading its influence throughout the region. The supporters' club was highly active, with new branches forming in Shotley, Bildeston and Braintree, and plans laid down to establish others in Harwich, Felixstowe and Woodbridge. As ever, a high proportion of Town's support was based in surrounding areas, as opposed to the town itself.

John Bloom, a schoolboy fan from Old Newton, recalls those salad days with affection. 'I would be given five bob by my parents and would set off for Haughley station on matchdays. The fare to Ipswich was around 9d, it was 1s 6d to get in and a programme was 4d. We would go early and make a day of it, getting to the ground a long time before kick-off, to wander around, hoping to get players' autographs. Loads of others would also get there early and someone always seemed to have a ball, so massive kickabouts would develop on the practice pitch behind the stand – something like 40-a-side. The surface was hard-packed mud from the players' training during the week. I would often take a wooden stool with me to get a better view of the game. Occasionally the bigger matches were all-ticket and that meant we had to go to a reserve game the week before to get our tickets. We didn't mind though, because football was our only entertainment and pastime – there was nothing else really. Crowds always seemed huge in those days. Most of us would wear a scarf knitted by our mum and many would have huge wooden rattles, which these days would probably be banned. Most of the crowd seemed to favour bulky great duffle coats with wooden buttons. I had one and I'd get home and find the hood was full of rubbish that the bloke behind had put in.

'Crawford and Phillips were the biggest heroes because of their goalscoring. Crawford has this distinctive way of running, he sort of swaggered. Phillips' shooting was just so fierce. One goalkeeper was daft enough to get in the way of a Phillips penalty and I remember him standing there wringing his hands in pain, the shot had been so hard. A great talking point among fans was always that strange patch on the back of Phillips' head. And one thing that always raised a cheer was trainer Forsyth running on with his magic sponge, water sploshing everywhere. He was an ancient-looking chap, and looked even older than "Sticks" Leadbetter! Town did so well in Division One and made the big sides seem ordinary There was a lot less information and coverage in those days – we just relied on newspapers. That's why it took other teams so long to work out how to combat Town, too.'

Although 1961-62 crowds were boisterous and noisy, there was little chanting or singing. Occasionally there'd be a burst of '2-4-6-8 who do we appreciate…' and later in the season 'Keep Right On To The End of the Road' became popular, but most of the noise was made by individuals shouting things out to amuse those around them. Says Bloom: 'You would get jeering at the referee, but it was rarely obscene and was usually stuff like "go home ref" or "on yer bike, ref".

'Another commonly-heard shout was directed at chairman Cobbold, enquiring what he'd done with all the money. The smaller lads would sometimes be passed overhead and allowed to stand at the front so they could see. When crowds were really big they would let some of us sit on the grass in front of the wall. On the terraces it was common to find you couldn't see all the game, but the stool would help. Crowds were very male-oriented and there were few women and it seemed like everyone smoked. You could get a cup of tea, but the toilets and other facilities were very poor in those days. Down in the corner where the players' ran out, they would let invalid carriages and wheelchairs park at the front. It used to raise a big cheer when during the game the ball would thump against the little blue invalid cars.'

England sweltered amid a heatwave in early September and Town's red-hot form against Burnley was maintained. West Brom were turned over 3-1 on their own ground, with supporter John Finch recording in his journal: 'The helter-skelter approach of WBA was in complete contrast to the cool Ipswich approach, which was very wise in the amazing heat. It was almost too hot to watch, let alone play in.' Three days later and another humid evening saw nearly 25,000 squeeze into Portman Road to see Town overcome Blackburn 2-1. All the goals came in the first period, with Town's second an absolute peach, Phillips rocketing home Leadbetter's pass after a neat move. World Cup referee Ken Aston infuriated Town by letting Rovers back into the game with a penalty for Baxter's challenge on England winger Bryan Douglas. The ground was heaving with its biggest gate in over seven years and the St John Ambulance brigade was kept busy as the heat took its toll.

The goals continued to flow and a fourth successive win, 4-1 over a poor Birmingham side in the second week of September, took Town to the heady heights of fourth. Ramsey's deep-lying wingers flummoxed the Midlanders and John Finch reckoned that Roy Stephenson, who'd looked rather ordinary earlier on, 'was now proving some winger.' Leadbetter, enjoying his 250th game for the club, managed to fool the burly opposing defenders into feeling sorry for such a 'spindly-legged fellow', according to Finch, but by the end he had made them change their attitude.

Revenge was gained over Manchester City with a 4-2 win in the League Cup, a competition still in its infancy and attracting far lower crowds than the League games. Everton then brought Town's winning run to a grinding halt. With Burnley having gone top in early September – a position they would occupy until the end of March – Town found themselves seven points adrift of the top after their 2-5 hammering at Goodison Park. New full-back Compton was given his stiffest test yet by a rampant Billy Bingham and was often totally outmanoeuvered by the Irish winger. Town couldn't cope with Everton's attacking flair and it was their poorest display thus far in the top flight. Due to a leg injury, Roy Bailey had been replaced in goal by Wilf Hall, and the new boy looked nervous and tentative.

On the same evening that 800 demonstrators were arrested in London for the biggest 'ban the bomb' demo yet seen, Town bounced back by picking up a hard-earned point at Blackburn. Phillips' late equaliser went in off his face, leaving him dazed and unaware he'd even scored. At the end of this week, Town's bogey side Fulham came to Portman Road, and according to supporter John Finch's meticulous journal: 'They were being led a merry dance by Crawford and Phillips, until Johnny Haynes put his stamp on the game and began dictating play. I don't mind when he does this for England but I do object when he comes here and gives us a lesson.' Reportedly now the first English footballer to be earning £100 a week, Haynes' passing was masterful and he gave Town a real lesson as he inspired the Cottagers' 4-2 win.

Workmanlike Sheffield Wednesday were next up, but the Owls had nobody to dictate proceedings in the manner of Haynes. Town, playing in an unfamiliar change kit of red, built up a 3-1 lead before half-time. Against Fulham, Town's fans had greeted Haynes' superb passing with complete silence (perhaps it was his air of arrogance and the size of his wallet?), but in contrast, at Hillsborough, the Sheffield public were generous in their approval of Ted Phillips' shooting. They clearly enjoyed seeing this raw-boned country boy having a go at every possible opportunity. Phillips' reputation was spreading and both friend and foe alike loved the spectacular sight of him having a crack from distance. Owls fans applauded warmly when he let fly in the early stages and struck a post. Likewise after the interval when he got clear and thrashed home what he later described as his fiercest shot of his career, to round off a fine 4-1 win. One young Town fan, Rod Cross, would later recall the awe and excitement of seeing a Phillips rocket hit an opponent on the side of the head and knock him cold for several minutes.

Although Ipswich had by now conceded four or more goals in three separate games, the goals were also pouring in at the other end and Town fans were loving it. A noticeable feature of home games was the increased volume of noise now coming from the new-look North Stand. It seemed like the Churchman's End's reputation as the only section to make any real noise was in jeopardy. Up to this point, Town had always preferred kicking towards Churchman's, because of the atmosphere, but now the tide was turning and within a few years the North Stand would take over 'lead vocals'.

In October, Jimmy 'Chisel' Forsyth passed 500 games as the club's trainer. The Scot had arrived from Millwall back in 1950, having earlier learned his First Aid skills with the Civil Defence in London. Physiotherapy was a word rarely heard in football in 1961 and a trainer's favourite tool was his magic sponge. Nevertheless, wee Jimmy had an impressive kit-box at his disposal for 1961-62. Its contents make interesting reading: three triangular bandages for fractures, methylated spirits for ankle injuries, smelling salts for concussion, antiseptic for cuts, adrenalin plugs for nosebleeds and various anti-irritant ointments as well as the sponge and water. Jimmy seemed well-equipped, but his kit-box was overshadowed by that of Bert Sproston, the former England player who was head trainer at Bolton. Bert's contained glucose, haircream, Elastoplast, liver salts, insoles, bandages, cotton wool, bottles of iodine, TCP, hot oil, olive oil, acraflavine, lead opium, glycerine, thymol, sal volatile and gentian violet. One trainer of the time who went even further was Dawson Walker, sponge-man to Clyde and Scotland, who carried with him dentistry pliers and chloroform, in case he needed to pull a tooth in a game. Walker also used an improvised water-polo cap to help keep head bandages in place.

After many years of heavy footballs and sturdy ankle-supporting boots, kit was being brought up to date at a fast rate. Balls and boots were generally lighter than those of the 1950s. The favoured boots of 1961-62 were the Mansfield Hotspur Continental, which retained the hard toe-cap (retail price £3 5s 11d), while top of the range across Europe was the Val Sport Braziliana, a lightweight model with innovative padding, designed in Italy and selling at £7 9s 6d.

Ipswich took the chance to relax from League action a little too literally at Swansea in the League Cup second round. They found themselves 0-3 down to the Second Division outfit within 24 minutes. A few firm words at the interval from Ramsey inspired a second-half comeback to gain a replay at Portman Road. In this second encounter, the game followed a similar pattern to the first. The Swans took a two-goal lead, only to capitulate again after the break and concede another three.

Town made up for these erratic cup displays with wonderful League victories over West Ham and Tottenham in October. In front of the best gate since 1938, West Ham were trounced 4-2, all six goals coming in a half-hour period during the thrilling second half. Crawford poached two and recalled that the result helped win a group of players a handy pay-out on the 'pools'. He recalled they did a 40-1 fixed odds bet for four home wins, going for three home 'bankers' plus the Ipswich game. All four came up and paid out handsomely.

A fortnight later things got even better when a record crowd of 28,778 squeezed into Portman Road to see reigning double winners Spurs. It was a perfect afternoon for football and the ground was packed hours before the start. Little Welsh winger Cliff Jones twice headed the visitors ahead, but Town battled back each time. Two minutes after Crawford's nicely taken second equaliser, he brought the house down by netting a goal of style and nonchalance, to put Ipswich ahead for the first time. Rarely has a goal been so joyously received at Portman Road and the wide-eyed scorer surveyed the euphoria around him and simply shrugged his shoulders, as if to say how easy it all was. The fans just lapped it up. Bailey made a miraculous save and both sides hit the woodwork late on in this thriller. The result took Town above Spurs in the table, which delighted Ramsey, in particular, as a former Spurs player. Typically, though, he refused to get carried away and told reporters he'd actually enjoyed the West Ham game more.

As well as the 3-2 scoreline, one particular Town fan had an extra reason to celebrate the victory over mighty Spurs. In order to win a ten-shilling bet, John Eastwood had to be the first person to get into the ground before the start. Knowing a record crowd was on the cards, and that many would arrive very early, young John decided he would have to get there on the Friday night. He recalls: 'I sat outside the North Stand all night. It was very, very cold and by the time dawn broke my coat was covered in frost. An elderly policeman came round at regular intervals during the ordeal and about 6 in the morning he persuaded me to go to the railway station for a cup of tea – I hadn't even brought a flask. But by the time I got back a few other early birds had arrived and started to form a queue. Fortunately my friendly bobby returned and explained to them that I'd been there all night, thus restoring me to my place at the head of the line. It was a hard-earned ten shillings, but well worth it.' One fan highly upset at missing the Spurs game was schoolboy Elvin King: 'Spurs were a huge team then and it was a massive blow to miss this game because I was playing in a Minor Cup game for Woolverstone Juniors. It made things even worse when we lost that game by double figures.'

The only aspect of the Spurs game that disappointed the *EADT*'s Alan Everitt was the way the Tottenham players celebrated their goals. Noting that scorer Jones was actually kissed by his team-mates in a very unmanly manner, the indignant Everitt called for a halt to such displays. Surely a handshake was sufficient, he thundered.

The slaying of Tottenham naturally increased the attention paid to Ipswich by the national media. The pressbox was packed for the following game, a 1-1 draw at Blackpool, and one correspondent, anxious (like Ramsey) not to get carried away, analysed the Ipswich phenomenon thus: 'Ipswich are not exciting; they do not make the pulses race. Simply, they are eleven men doing their job professionally, blessed with a rich team spirit, backing each other, covering each other's faults and playing to their strong points.'

The club was bubbling with enthusiasm and nobody was enjoying life more than chairman John Cobbold, who played a typical prank during the visit to Blackpool. After spotting a man on the seafront with a performing monkey, the Town chairman asked to borrow the animal for a few hours. He then produced the monkey to a stunned Blackpool boardroom, introducing it as the latest addition to the Ipswich Town board of directors.

A Villa player (left) trots off. Nelson (right) and the fans don't yet know if Town are champions

Jimmy Leadbetter is chaired from the pitch following the final whistle against Aston Villa

A post-match interview with Bailey, Elsworthy, Carberry, Phillips and Leadbetter

Another post-match interview, this time beside the cricket pavilion that served as changing rooms

Chapter Seven

~ *Hanging in There* ~
November 1961 – February 1962

On Guy Fawkes weekend 1961 the sparks began to fly at the top of Division One. Burnley opened up a three-point gap at the top, while everybody's favourite country cousins – Ipswich Town – moved into the top three for the first time. Never mind that an undistinguished single-goal victory over Nottingham Forest had put Town there, for this was heady stuff for Suffolk folk. On his 200th appearance, Ted Phillips smote home the game's only goal in the first half and the nearest thing to another goal came late in the game when Roy Bailey dived to save a Calvin Palmer penalty. The jostling for fresh air at the top of the table continued a week later, with Town slipping back to fifth after going down 0-2 at Molineux, where they were handicapped by the early departure of an injured Roy Stephenson. The remaining ten men worked like demons to keep the snarling Wolves at bay, but ultimately cracked in heartbreaking fashion in the closing minutes, conceding goals to teenage wingers Terry Wharton, making his debut, and Alan Hinton.

England boss Walter Winterbottom took in the First Division's new boys for himself when Town entertained mighty Manchester United at Portman Road. The Red Devils' first ever visit to Suffolk saw them humbled to the tune of 4-1 and by the final stages Town's superiority was almost embarrassing. John Elsworthy recalls: 'Late in the game we were winning so comfortably that I thought I'd try something different from a free-kick. As a youngster in Wales I'd played rugby and had been good at conversions, and had learned how to put back-spin on a ball and make it dip. With this free-kick I struck it just right and it dipped towards goal like a spinning conversion attempt, and spun right up Dave Gaskell's arm and over his shoulder into the net.' To the naked eye it looked like Gaskell had made a dreadful misjudgment of an easy ball, but Elsworthy insists it was all entirely deliberate.

Ray Crawford was widely expected to receive a call-up for the Football League representative side in November, but when the squad was named without him, Town followers were left scratching their heads in bewilderment. Shortly afterwards, disbelief turned to delight when Winterbottom picked Crawford for his country against Northern Ireland, thus making him the East Anglian region's first full England international. The honour was well deserved and another feather in Ipswich's cap, but sadly the game at Wembley was a poor spectacle in front of a low crowd. Although he laid on England's goal for Bobby Charlton in the 1-1 draw, Crawford hit the bar with an easy chance and didn't look his usual self without the service of a Leadbetter or a Stephenson. While Crawford was struggling under the twin towers, his team-mates were up at Villa Park, overcoming Joe Mercer's side in an entertaining 3-2 League Cup victory.

Leader of the (Labour) Opposition Hugh Gaitskell was among the crowd who witnessed a never-to-be-forgotten goal by Ted Phillips at Cardiff on the final Saturday of November. The hard-bitten regulars in the Ninian Park pressbox described it as the most remarkable goal ever seen at the famous stadium. Even by Phillips' standards, this was a real thunderbolt of a shot. Only eight minutes were on the clock when he belted the ball goalwards from a tight angle, at least 30 yards out. It dipped and swerved wildly as it jetted into the net past disbelieving 17-year-old rookie keeper Dilwyn John. No wonder that John spent the remainder of the game looking a nervous wreck. Phillips was now regularly producing long-range drives of such extraordinary power that opposition fans could only stand and applaud in admiration. He was helped by the fact that the old leather balls of the 1950s had by now been replaced by lighter, plastic-coated models and some goalkeepers went on record as saying these lighter balls 'did things' in the air when hit from distance. Frightened goalkeepers and lighter balls – it was music to big Ted's ears.

The 3-0 triumph at Cardiff pushed Town into second place in the table behind Burnley, who were by now in red-hot form and being widely tipped to win the title, even though the season had yet to reach its halfway point. Having reached the summit in early September, the attractive Clarets' side had won ten of their first fourteen games, scoring 43 goals in the process, 27 of them away from home. Although they would inevitably slacken this sort of pace later on, they nevertheless headed the table throughout the winter and would not get caught until the final day of March. But more of that later.

One of the revelations in the Town side as Christmas approached was left-half Elsworthy, a commanding figure in the midfield. He possessed an excellent eye for a pass and a laid-back, unhurried style that would later be the trademark of the West Ham and England maestro Trevor Brooking. 'Without Elsworthy we are like a one-winged chicken,' wrote one appreciative fan to the *Football Star.* The big man had certainly adapted more effectively than expected to top-flight football after twelve years playing in the lower divisions and overcoming several serious injuries. Performing at this high level was the crowning glory for a popular, unassuming figure who might have made a career in cricket had it not been for the excellent network of contacts of former Town boss Scott Duncan.

Elsworthy recalled his start at Ipswich: 'After the war I was an amateur on Newport County's books and working in an office in the Cardiff docks area. Newport's coach Billy Owen had worked with Scott Duncan at Manchester United and tipped him off about me. Duncan came to see me and offered me £7 per week – £5 in the summer – plus a lump sum of £25, to sign professional for Ipswich. I agreed, but shortly afterwards the Cardiff City manager came to my home and said they'd match Ipswich's offer and allow me to continue working part-time in the office. They were a bigger club, but I stuck to my word and joined Ipswich. All this came just a few days after I'd had a trial with Glamorgan in their indoor nets and was offered a contract as a fast bowler. As football went on for nine months a year, and cricket for only three, I opted for football.

'I went to Portman Road but after three months had to head off for National Service in the RAF at West Kirby. As I was on Town's books, they soon allowed me to be stationed at RAF Mildenhall, which is 38 miles from Ipswich. I was picked for the Bomber Command team and we did well, and this meant Air Vice-Marshal Hesketh heard about me. He was very keen on sport and said if ever I needed time off to play for Ipswich he would personally authorise it. For two years I had to get a bus from the air base to Bury St Edmunds and then a train to Ipswich on matchdays, returning to the camp after the game.

'Manager Scott Duncan was a dour man who was clever with money. He was not scientific about his football really. When Alf Ramsey replaced him in 1955 we'd been relegated and we were in a mess. It was a real shambles – Ken Malcolm had been played in about eight different positions, for example. I had been moved from inside-forward to half-back, although I found I preferred it here anyway. Alf didn't try to change my way of playing, he let me get on with it. It was the same with most of the others really – only Phillips and Crawford seemed to get lots of instructions from him. Alf treated you very respectfully and never ran you down. He was the first tracksuit manager really and a great thinker. He was always one step ahead of the opposition. In life you sometimes come across someone who is a bit special and he was like that.

'The Portman Road pitch was always in wonderful condition and lovely to pass a ball on. Sometimes people would ask me why didn't I shoot more often, but I would say why shoot from 30 yards when I can get the ball to Ted Phillips who will shoot from twenty?' Reaching the top flight was a real triumph for Elsworthy, for at one point in the late 1950s his career seemed over. 'In a game with Rotherham, a defender tackled me hard and a piece of cane from his shin-guard pierced my shin. It didn't hurt much at the time, but it subsequently caused a thrombosis and I had to have a spell in hospital. The first doctor said I'd be all right to play again, but a second one took over and he reckoned I was finished. At that point I took over a grocery shop in Ipswich as security for the future – but eventually I got the go-ahead to play again and continued running the shop anyway. I never looked back after that and had my best footballing years after the injury, when I was around 30.'

Had Elsworthy played in a different era, he would surely have gained dozens of caps for Wales. 'I wasn't playing for a fashionable club you see, and in those days if you didn't get watched often enough – especially in home games – then you wouldn't get picked. And Ipswich was a long way for them to come and see me.'

Elsworthy recalls that Ramsey told his men from the outset that if they could amass 24 points by Christmas they would be safe from the relegation that most experts had predicted would be their fate. The thrilling 5-2 hammering of Chelsea at Portman Road on 2 December saw Town pass that 24-point mark, meaning the pundits were eating their words with 22 games still to be played. With relegation avoided, the players could now really enjoy themselves. A young Chelsea side, marshalled by manager Ted Drake, put on a decent display that afternoon, playing some clever football, but their defence had no answer to Town's ruthless forwards. Rampant Crawford blasted a hat-trick and the West London glamour boys were left empty-handed and marooned at the bottom of the table.

Town suffered disruption the following weekend when Billy Baxter sent a message through from his barracks that he would be unable to get leave to play for Town – the first time this had happened this season. His commanding officer's parade rehearsal was taking place at the same time as Town's game at Aston Villa. It was bad news for Town as Baxter had been playing superbly alongside Andy Nelson, but the cloud had a silver lining for Ipswich-born reserve Dennis Thrower. The 24-year-old was called up to replace Baxter for what would have been his first game in the first team for five years. It had been a long wait in the wings for the talented local product but, sadly for him, Baxter obtained a very late reprieve and joined the squad in the nick of time. It was typical of the spirit within the squad that Baxter felt genuinely sorry for Thrower over this, and apologised for the turn of events. As things turned out, Thrower was better off on the sidelines, for Villa's Derek Dougan and Peter McParland led Town a merry dance and, even with Baxter, the defence looked shaky in a 0-3 defeat. The slump continued two days later as Blackburn powered four goals past Roy Bailey in the fourth round of the League Cup.

The turn of the year was looming and a good display the following week was imperative to get the show back on the road. However, visitors Bolton made things difficult with some rugged, spoiling tactics which upset Town players and started the fans slow-handclapping. In the final ten minutes, with Town trailing to a Doug Holden goal, the crowd suddenly came to life after one foul too many by no-nonsense defender Syd Farrimond. Seemingly tired of moaning, the Churchman's End of the ground now began roaring Town forward. When a corner was won after 83 minutes the noise became deafening. Winger Stephenson took the kick and said later he felt the whole Churchman's Stand was taking it with him. He floated the ball over and Crawford, galvanised by the sudden change in atmosphere, raced in and cannoned into keeper Eddie Hopkinson. The keeper caught the ball and turned sideways to meet Crawford's challenge, staggering on the goalline but clinging onto the ball despite the hefty shoulder-charge. Town players and the crowd shouted for a goal and referee

Clements, who had a good view, agreed that the ball had been carried over the line. Bolton were incensed and claimed not only a foul by Crawford, but also that the ball never crossed the line anyway. Wanderers' resolve was now broken and five minutes later there were even more frenetic celebrations when Crawford hooked in the winner. Bolton's negative tactics had failed and they suffered further misery when forward Brian Pilkington broke his leg in the last minute.

The recently-retired Bolton and England centre-forward Nat Lofthouse, famous for his own shoulder charges, wrote about Crawford's controversial equaliser in a syndicated newspaper column the following week: 'I'm all against changing the rules. What is more, I think you will find the majority of Great Britain's top goalkeepers agree with me. In my opinion it is perfectly legitimate to challenge the goalkeeper, not only where there is a chance it might produce a goal but also when the goalkeeper is one-footed and you want to make him use his "dummy" foot for a clearance.' Crawford's challenge had certainly been no worse than many that had gone before by Bolton's defenders. Indeed, some observers suspected the ref allowed the goal to stand partly to even things up a little. Town skipper Nelson said afterwards: 'One cannot feel sorry for an outfit who adopted such methods, which are doing little to get back the missing fans.'

Legend has it that Bolton also proved tricky customers to deal with in the boardroom. Town chairman John Cobbold is said to have greeted his opposite number – a bluff character called Alderman Entwhistle – by offering him a cigar. 'I've never smoked in my life,' came the indignant reply. The Alderman then also turned down the offer of a glass of whisky: 'Never has alcohol passed my lips,' he said. This was all too much for the hospitable Cobbold, who announced briskly: 'Then sir, we have absolutely nothing in common.'

The Bolton match still makes supporter Steve Prentice chuckle 40 years later. Then a 14-year-old paperboy, earning 15 shillings a week at Eaton's Newsagents in Nacton Road, he had to dash back from Saturday matches to deliver the *Evening Star* and *Football Star* to houses in the Clapgate Lane area. On matchdays he would leave his bike at the newsagent's and travel to the ground on the back of his dad's BSA B40 motorbike. 'We parked on the old livestock market for a quick getaway and stood at the back of the Chicken Run area, next to the entrance on the halfway line. As I was quite small, I stood on a rickety old stool and my dad Bill would annoy everyone by continually smoking Player's Whisky Flake in his beloved pipe.

'It was a cold, grey afternoon against Bolton, who were a big, physical team. As the game progressed, my father became increasingly exasperated with the visitors' time-wasting and with a few minutes left decided he could take no more punishment and announced we were leaving. I pleaded with him to stay to the final whistle but after a brief argument he stormed off leaving me on my own. Immediately after he left the stadium, Crawford equalised and then amid great scenes of jubilation scored a dramatic winner with virtually the last kick of the match. Bolton had got their just desserts and I had to make a mad dash to Electric House to catch a No 2 bus for the newsagent's, where proprietor's wife Mrs Paston was extremely displeased with my late arrival. After rushing round delivering the papers, I got home and my mother informed me that father was sulking quietly in the front room, puffing away at his pipe in the dark. He hadn't even listened to *Sports Report* to confirm his grief and check his pools coupon. When I burst into the room telling him we had pulled off an amazing last-ditch 2-1 victory, he wouldn't believe me and warned me of the dire consequences of winding him up. I even fetched neighbour Cyril Rollings to confirm my story, but it was not accepted until he saw the result in that evening's *Football Star*. Recovery was swift and he very soon disappeared in good humour with mother in the direction of their favourite Saturday night whist drive at the Boys Brigade HQ in Hogarth Road. The following morning he was persuaded to visit the shop and explain why I had reported late for duty. Newsagent Harold Paston, himself a regular supporter, was very sympathetic and my weekend was complete.'

The defensive frailties displayed in the previous two away games were evident again at Manchester City, on a bone-hard, semi-frozen pitch. Wearing their red strip again, Town's attack misfired and gave 38-year-old German-born keeper Bert Trautmann little trouble. At the other end, Neil Young – who was 21 years Trautmann's junior – posed Town all sorts of problems and netted just after half-time to kill the game at 3-0. Three days later, on Boxing Day, Jimmy Leadbetter's run of 156 consecutive games was ended by a knee injury, but his teammates secured their eighth successive home win when Crawford shot past Gordon Banks to sink Leicester 1-0 in freezing cold conditions.

The weather deteriorated across the UK on New Year's Eve 1961 and by late morning that day no fewer than 31 of the day's League fixtures had been called off due to snow and slush – a new record for a single day. Town set off by train for their away game at Leicester but after reaching St Pancras Station learned that it was off. Alf Ramsey wondered why the pitch inspection could not have been carried out earlier before his party had set off from Suffolk. 'It was a stupid waste of £25 travelling expenses,' he moaned. Andy Nelson and a couple of team-mates stopped off on the return journey and visited Layer Road, Colchester, where one of only twelve surviving games was being played. Although they witnessed the home side chalk up a club-record 9-1 win over Bradford City, Nelson announced himself unimpressed by the display of Town's Essex neighbours. Perhaps the Ipswich skipper's remarks were a deliberate attempt to introduce some spice to his new newspaper column, which was being run in the *Football Star*. In taking on this job, Nelson had insisted he would not need the services of a ghost writer. He carefully composed every word himself and obediently dropped his copy into the paper's Carr Street offices every Wednesday afternoon. His new media high profile was mirrored by the handsome new mode of transport he obtained around Christmas – a smart Ford Anglia saloon.

As 1962 dawned, Burnley were still in pole position in Division One, with Town having slipped back to fourth. The Clarets brushed aside Manchester United 4-1 at Old Trafford and at home they pummelled Aston Villa 3-0, Sheffield Wednesday 4-0 and Sheffield United 4-2. Supplied by the skilful Jimmy McIlroy, their England duo Ray Pointer and John Connelly tore defences to shreds. Manchester City and West Ham both conceded six at Turf Moor, while Birmingham collapsed 0-7 there in early February. This form, coupled with the inconsistency of title-holders Spurs, suggested the championship was on its way to East Lancashire.

Attention turned to the FA Cup in January and it took Ipswich three games to dispose of Second Division Luton Town in round three. The second replay was staged at Highbury, and Town were quick to punish a blunder that Hatters' skipper Bob Morton committed even before the game started. Morton won the toss and chose unwisely to kick against a fierce wind. Using the wind to their advantage, Ipswich were three up within sixteen minutes and there was no way back for Luton, who ultimately succumbed by 5-1. It was handsome revenge for the 2-5 cup defeat at Luton's hands three years earlier. Goalkeeper Wilf Hall replaced injured Bailey for the Highbury replay and was delighted and relieved when things went well – for just a week or two earlier his copybook had been well and truly blotted when he conceded a total of 27 goals in four successive reserve games. The reserves were certainly putting on some top-class entertainment around this period, for their eighteen league games had produced no fewer than 107 goals – an average of around six per match.

Supporter Jim Crane looks back at the winter of 1961-62 with great fondness and recalls how he and his pals would travel to away games by coach and to home games by train from Haughley village: 'It didn't cost a huge amount in those days and I never missed a game, home or away, from the age of twelve right up to about 30. I worked for a company called Stramit Boards and luckily our boss, Cecil Bugg, was a big Ipswich fan. He was willing to be flexible about letting us get to midweek games and sometimes would even bump up our bonus payments if Town were doing well. His son Alec later played in goal for the club in the late 1960s. Our home match routine was to get the 1.30 train from Haughley to Ipswich. I always wore my smart blue suit with a dickie bow. You would always see the same people on the train. Some of the Town fans had got on earlier at Newmarket and Cambridge. Around 200 of us would get on at the Haughley stop. Town got very healthy support from the outlying villages in those days and always have done since. It was bad news when the Beeching [railway] cuts came along in 1963 and closed our station, for loads of football fans used it. Life was different in those days and the players would come out before the game and stroll around the pitch and sign autographs and chat. As the 1961-62 season got going we realised that all the teams were good in this League: even Chelsea, who were at the bottom, played really well and were an attractive young side. But Ipswich were playing a different game to the rest and their tactics messed with the opposition.'

Ipswich played only two League games in January 1962 – a 3-0 home win over West Brom and a lethargic 1-3 reverse at Birmingham. The month was dominated by FA Cup action and the victory over Luton saw Town drawn away to neighbours Norwich in the fourth round. This tussle generated huge interest and while almost 40,000 squeezed into Carrow Road, others took advantage of new technology to watch the game on closed circuit TV at the Baths Hall in Ipswich. Town, used to the immaculate Portman Road playing surface, looked a little tentative on bumpy Carrow Road and were happy to escape with a 1-1 draw. One supporter reported that on leaving the Canaries ground he was 'kicked in the pants' and had his hat knocked off after suggesting loudly that Norwich should harvest the sugar beet from their pitch and get rid of the bumps.

Despite dominating the tense replay, Town were beaten by a Terry Allcock goal in the dying moments. An aggregate crowd of 69,986 watched the two ties and the blue contingent simply couldn't believe they'd been beaten by a mid-table Second Division outfit who'd been outplayed for so long in the replay. With Burnley making progress in the Cup, at least Town could now tackle the League programme with fewer distractions. The Cup defeat created a blank Saturday in February and this was filled when German side TSV Alemannia Aachen were invited over for a friendly. A telegram had arrived to confirm the arrangements but, with nobody at Portman Road able to read German, office staff were flummoxed and left guessing over the contents. The Germans were the first foreign side to play at the ground since 1937 and their side of part-timers, which included a film star, were easily beaten 5-0 in front of 10,000.

A few days after Decca famously turned down a 'Merseybeat combo' from Liverpool called The Beatles, Town got their act together in the League again by trouncing Everton 4-2. This wiped away some of the misery of the Cup defeat and supporter John Finch recorded that 'Ipswich buckled down and swept the formidable Everton side off their feet. They have now beaten all the fancied teams and if they can only keep some consistency they would well have a chance of topping the League.' Victory was clinched against Harry Catterick's men with a wonderful Crawford goal on his 150th appearance – a piece of exquisite finishing at the end of a move he started himself.

According to official figures, 1962 saw a total of 750 die as a result of London smog, but the capital held no fears for Ipswich Town. They remained unbeaten in five trips there, with the first being a 2-1 success at Fulham that was more comfortable than the scoreline suggests. Even a magnificent Alan Mullery goal failed to distract Town and the Cottagers were sent tumbling to their ninth successive loss. This was followed by a far more exciting contest at West Ham, where defensive errors by Town proved decisive. Mistakes by the normally reliable Nelson and Bailey were both punished by goals, but Phillips thrashed home a penalty to save Town a point in a 2-2 draw.

During February an East Anglian schoolboy claimed a world record for doing the new dance-craze, the Twist, for 33-hours non-stop. Town fans wished such energetic displays could have been transferred to the lean and wiry frame of inside-left Ted Phillips. Since early December the big No 10 had been mysteriously off-form and his flow of spectacular goals had dried up. His barren spell became a talking point in both national and local press, and when broadcaster John Arlott asked Ramsey how much longer he would persevere with Ted after nearly three months of poor form, the stubborn manager replied 'Another three months'. Ramsey was also angry at local sports editor Alan Everitt, who wrote that Phillips' form had 'completely disintegrated'. The player was much-loved by the fans as the only Suffolk lad in their team, but his off-colour displays soon led to a spate of barracking and cat-calls. Ramsey kept his nerve and refused to drop Phillips – and that faith would soon be repaid in a big way.

Conveyed by an Eastern National bus, the conquering heroes arrive on the Cornhill (May 1962)

Huge crowds congregate on Ipswich Cornhill to await their heroes

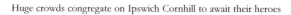

Alf Ramsey and John Cobbold watch Ipswich's Mayor, Mrs Charlotte Green, address the crowd

The cheers ring out as the open top bus arrives on the Cornhill (May 1962)

Skipper Andy Nelson hoists aloft the First Division Championship trophy on the Cornhill

Chapter Eight

~ *Rising from the Pack* ~

March-May 1962

At the beginning of March, Town found themselves in third place in Division One with a dozen League games remaining. Leaders Burnley had reached the quarter-finals of the FA Cup and consequently had games in hand. They remained hot favourites for the title and talk at Turf Moor was all about emulating Spurs by 'doing the double'. Town had already exceeded pre-season expectations and since the turn of the year had been able to enjoy their football, and this lack of inhibition often produced scintillating games – Sheffield United at home being a classic example.

Considering John Harris's side had gone sixteen matches without defeat and were also a top-six side, the contest was extraordinarily one-sided. Town attacked at will and, after a smart Doug Moran goal was followed by one from Jimmy Leadbetter with only 25 minutes gone, the result was never in doubt. Ray Crawford had a magnificent game, giving experienced defender Joe Shaw the run-around and scoring twice after the break. John Elsworthy recalls: 'As we came off the pitch, I remember Shaw asking me if we usually played as well as that. When I said we did, he said he seriously believed we could go on and win the League.'

Ramsey told the press that his team should have scored even more, but chose not to discuss the worrying situation over Ted Phillips. By now the fans had lost patience with Phillips' apparent lethargy and rock-bottom confidence. He was jeered during the Sheffield United game, even though he had 25 goals to his credit already over the season. However, that statistic hid the fact that he'd not looked himself for many weeks and had only hit the net twice in the last eleven League games, one of those a penalty. Ipswich fans were split over the Phillips issue, the majority rallying behind him and reacting angrily to the barracking and to the *EADT*'s calls for him to be dropped.

The other Sheffield outfit – Vic Buckingham's Wednesday – were in town six days later for the Ipswich public's first taste of 'pay night' soccer. The experiment was a huge success, with the Friday evening crowd revelling in the floodlit atmosphere, roaring Town forward in a marvellous contest that was much closer than the previous week's. Roy Stephenson commented that the level of support left him breathless, but fortunately he had enough puff with four minutes left to sprint through the visiting defence and net Crawford's pass to clinch a 2-1 win. This was the night that 'Keep Right On to the End of the Road' was adopted as an anthem by the fans, who sang it time and again towards the end, seemingly unworried that it was already the traditional terrace song at Birmingham City. It was stirring stuff and highly appropriate in view of the lateness of the goal that secured an eleventh successive home win.

So it was with great confidence that the Town party set off for what on paper looked the toughest challenge of the season – an away game at Tottenham. This midweek contest at the home of the League and Cup holders generated huge interest in Suffolk and events that night would still be talked about 40 years later. Among those who still go misty eyed at mention of the game is supporter Steve Prentice: 'I went to White Hart Lane as a fifteenth birthday treat and what a wonderful occasion it was. I had no problem getting time off from school, as PE teacher Mr Taylor was an avid Town fan himself. I played for my school team, Priory Heath, at a very muddy Westbourne on the same afternoon and I recall we were thrashed 0-7 and my old friend Maurice Plant scored four. After a quick shower, my parents whisked me to Ipswich station to catch the special train to Northumberland Park. At the match we stood at the front of the middle tier of the East Stand, close to half way. We arrived early and there was plenty of friendly banter between the supporters of both teams. There was no segregation and the extremely cocky Spurs fans rejected any possibility of an Ipswich victory and we were subjected to the usual 'country bumpkin' taunts. Once the match began it was a different story. Town dominated for long periods and ran out deserved winners.

'After the match the atmosphere among Ipswich fans walking towards the station was of sheer delight and satisfaction that our team had silenced those home supporters. We wondered if it was all a dream. Everyone linked arms and sang 'Glory, glory hallelujah and the Town go marching on', putting a slightly different slant on the famous Spurs song. My father, a lifelong supporter and one of the original club shareholders, always referred to this match as the club's finest hour and the performances of his two all-time favourites, Phillips and Elsworthy, had him really purring that night. I don't remember the journey home as apparently I slept through all the celebrations. The following day in the London papers only grudging praise was given to our heroes, but like Mr Ramsey we all knew our boys could match the very best in the land and something very special was happening in darkest Suffolk.'

Supporters who caught the BR special to Northumberland Park reckon the return fare of 13s 6d was one of the best investments they ever made. Many others went by coach, including Jim Crane, who recalls: 'At work I did the six-till-two shift to make sure I could catch the bus to Tottenham. It felt like a really big game as Spurs were the most complete side I'd ever seen, but we beat them well.' Fellow fan John Finch said at the time it was the most famous victory in the history of the club and the team's greatest ever display against the best team in Europe. It was certainly a proud night for Ramsey, a former Spurs favourite, and Elsworthy recalls it was the best he'd ever seen Town's forwards play. Phillips ended the debate over his form with a stunning display. 'Ted ran riot and Danny Blanchflower was completely ineffective,' says Elsworthy. 'We felt really good after that win – we'd fully deserved it.' Skipper Andy Nelson said the players had fought especially hard to give their manager a proud return to White Hart Lane.

On a rather threadbare pitch Town had got into their stride early. A neat early goal by Crawford rocked the champions briefly before Jimmy Greaves, just back from his Italian sojourn, equalised with a cheeky goal just 60 seconds later. With wing-halves Blanchflower and Tony Marchi pressing forward to join the attack, Town found themselves with big gaps to exploit. Nelson later said that Blanchflower's efforts to link with his forwards failed and the Town defence were able to break up attacks with ease. Two smart goals by the seemingly rejuvenated Phillips gave Town the points, and it might have been more than 3-1 as both Stephenson and Moran hit the bar.

On the same night, leaders Burnley drew at Cardiff, leaving themselves just a point ahead of Town, but with two games in hand. The national press still didn't seem particularly impressed by Town's title challenge and, in a letter to the *Football Star*, a Mr D Brabner suggested the football writers who underrated Town should be put in a leather bag, placed on the end of Felixstowe Pier and booted as far as possible out to sea by Ted Phillips.

Four days later Portman Road gave a rousing welcome home to the heroes of White Hart Lane, but – perhaps inevitably – the contest that followed was relatively disappointing. The run of successive home wins was ended in the last minute when Ray Charnley equalised for Blackpool after Town had led for 76 minutes through a Moran goal. Nelson reckoned the game had been as gruesome to play in as it had been to watch. Philllips, so soon after ending his barren spell, broke his thumb in colliding with keeper Bryan Harvey, allowing Dermot Curtis a rare look-in for the trip to Nottingham Forest a week later.

Crawford looked uncharacteristically subdued at the City Ground and Leadbetter, suffering a stomach upset, was also not his usual self. Town escaped with a 1-1 draw, a result that meant Burnley were left two points clear at the top, still with two games in hand. Four days later, with Filbert Street an absolute quagmire, Town battled hard and overcame Leicester 2-0, despite the home side having more of the play and creating far more chances.

On the final day of March, Burnley faced Fulham in an FA Cup semi-final, so Town knew a win over Wolves at Portman Road would put them top of the League for the first time. It proved a battle royal with Town unable to find their usual rhythm and meeting unexpected resistance from a Wolves side a dozen places below them. After being hauled down for a penalty, converted by Phillips, Crawford picked up a calf injury that rendered him a passenger out on the wing for most of the game. Nevertheless he was on hand to regain the lead after a spectacular Ron Flowers equaliser. Town somehow kept their noses ahead during a spell when they often looked second best, but the win needed to go top looked unlikely when Peter McParland equalised on the hour mark. Town's indomitable spirit saw them continue to plug away and, inspired by a remarkable double save by Roy Bailey, Moran popped up in the dying moments to slot a winner that brought the house down. The unthinkable had occurred – Ipswich were top of the League, with less than a month of the season left.

True, Burnley were just a point behind with *four* games in hand, but it was still a milestone to savour and particularly rewarding for the man who took up a local bookie's pre-season odds of 150-1 against Town ever topping the table. Supporter John Eastwood recalls the day well and in particular the vital Bailey save: 'With ten minutes left McParland lashed in a shot from outside the area which Bailey parried to the feet of the onrushing forwards. The ball was whacked goalwards good and hard and Roy had to launch himself from the ground to push it over the bar.'

After the game, England manager Walter Winterbottom called up Crawford for the international with Austria to replace injured Alan Peacock of Leeds. Crawford was also not fully fit, however, and it took lengthy bathing of his calf in the chilly North Sea at Felixstowe to get him ready for his Wembley date. Desperate to impress ahead of the announcement of the 1962 World Cup squad, Crawford managed a goal against Austria, but was not his usual mobile self. Unluckily, he would subsequently miss out on the squad for Chile and never played for his country again.

Crawford also missed Town's trip to a muddy Old Trafford in early April when Manchester United didn't meet with the resistance they might have expected from new League leaders. It was a demoralised looking Town who trooped off at the end of a 0-5 thrashing. Albert Quixall scored a superb hat-trick and Bobby Charlton hit the woodwork three times as Town's ten-match unbeaten run ended. The leadership was lost and winning the title looked a distant dream. Burnley were back on top thanks to a better goal-average and still had three games in hand. The United hammering had been like a bad dream, commented Nelson. In the muddy conditions Elsworthy picked up a muscle injury and was forced to miss the following game, against his home-town team, Cardiff.

The relegation-bound Welsh side attracted under 18,000 to Portman Road – a drop of nearly 6,000 on the previous home gate, which suggested that many fans had given up hopes of the title. The match was a poor spectacle and Town looked anxious, particularly when Barrie Hole crashed a shot against the bar early on, but nerves were settled when Moran tapped in an easy goal. It needed another remarkable late save by Bailey, from a Peter King volley, to allow Town to hang on for the win. With Burnley losing at home to Manchester United, Town dramatically found themselves top of the pile again.

Although Ramsey's lads had started to look a little vulnerable, it was clear that Burnley were faltering to an even worse degree. They seemed to be frittering away their games in hand and losing confi-

dence by the week. Meanwhile, the desperation on the Portman Road
terraces displayed during the Cardiff game was replaced by a carnival
atmosphere for the visit of Arsenal on Good Friday. The attendance
of 30,649 smashed the ground record and included a substantial
number from London. Robert Rackham, a Spurs fan who was fasci-
nated by the rise of Ipswich and determined to see this game, remembers coming up the A12 with a group of Arsenal fans. Although they
arrived very early, the place was already heaving and the gate they
queued at closed before they could get through. This caused a rumpus
among a group of Teddy Boy Arsenal fans, who suspected their mode
of dress was responsible for the shut-out. They were certainly not the
only people turned away, however, and some put life and limb at risk
by climbing onto the roof of a stand in a bid to see the game.

The tension seemed to have a negative effect on Ipswich and,
prompted by the excellent George Eastham, George Swindin's side
went 2-0 ahead after an hour's play. The game changed completely
after Crawford was hauled down for a penalty, converted by Phillips,
and from then on an equaliser looked inevitable. It came amid fren-
zied celebrations five minutes from time, from the boot of Leadbetter
after a bizarre goalmouth scramble. Supporter John Finch wrote in his
journal: 'The atmosphere all through was electric and spectators were
invading the pitch as goals were scored, something that had never happened here before.' But Burnley beat Blackpool that same afternoon
and returned to the top on goal-average.

Twenty-four hours later Town headed into London to face lowly
Chelsea and again nerves seemed to get the better of them. This time
tiredness was inevitably a factor, too, and Town fans watched in horror as the home side cruised into a two-goal lead before half-time.
Another dramatic rally saw a point saved, Town riding their luck and
equalising from the spot after John Mortimore unaccountably handled. Burnley, by now having reached the Cup final, lost at Sheffield
United, so Town's fortunate point saw them reclaim the leadership.
Spurs were beaten at home by West Brom and were now out of the
race. The three top teams had slipped up so often lately, that one wondered if any of them really wanted the title. Frankly, Town hadn't
looked the part for more than a month and Alan Hoby of the *Sunday
Express* wrote: 'I wish I could say Ipswich looked championship material. I cannot. But, of course, I am probably wrong.'

The third fixture over the four-day holiday weekend was Town's penultimate game of the campaign – the difficult-looking trip to Arsenal on Easter Monday. The weather was hot across the UK and horrendous traffic jams were reported everywhere, described as the worst in UK motoring history. Town certainly turned up the heat at Highbury and were brimming with confidence after getting off to a dream start, scoring two goals in the first twenty minutes through Phillips and Crawford. Despite playing with a pain-killing injection, Crawford sealed the win at 3-0 late in the second half with arguably Town's best goal of the entire season, a cracking drive after nutmegging Terry Neill.

Former 'A' team player Mick Banthorpe, recalls that day with pleasure: 'I was asked to guest for a YMCA side in a friendly at Kingston. As this was a morning kick-off, a couple of us decided to go to the big game at Highbury afterwards. After a few unsuccessful hitchhiking attempts we got into central London and on to Highbury via bus and tube. We left our hold-alls in a friendly local British Legion club and joined the Ipswich fans behind the goal. To celebrate the superb 3-0 win we went to the Tooting Castle pub, south of the river, for a knees-up. It was a brilliant night – gallons of beer and a noisy trip home. The driver of our bus entered into the spirit of things but insisted that if anyone felt ill they should make their way to the front of the bus so any "diced carrots" would be ejected out of the open door. In those days there were no Health and Safety rules dealing with football fans being sick out of moving buses. Supporter Kenny Smith took the driver's advice along the Embankment and was sick in the same direction as the Thames flowing from Putney to Mortlake. As we passed the great City institutions Ken suddenly cried out that he'd lost his false teeth, which had gone out the door as well. His teeth must have laid beside the Thames for weeks, grinning just like the fans of the team who would become champions.'

While Town were hammering mighty Arsenal, Burnley struggled to earn a point at Blackpool. This left Town on 54 points with one game left and Burnley two points behind but with a better goal-average and two games remaining. The title was definitely bound for either Turf Moor or Portman Road and – despite their recent shaky form – Burnley remained slight favourites in many people's eyes as their fate was still in their own hands. If they won both remaining games – at home to relegated Chelsea and away to Sheffield Wednesday – they would be champions whatever Town did at home to Aston Villa. From Ipswich's point of view the equation was simple – they needed to beat Villa and for Burnley to drop just one point from their two games. The bookies vacillated, with most settling on title odds of 4-5 on, for both clubs. However, *The Sporting Life* reckoned Ipswich were favourites, pointing out that Burnley's forthcoming FA Cup final was a major factor: 'The finalists normally like to take things easy but Burnley cannot. On Saturday they receive Chelsea, which should not prove too difficult but then only five days before Wembley they face the battle of their lives when they visit Sheffield Wednesday in what may well be the title decider,' wrote the *Life*'s correspondent. The *EADT* calculated that there were eighteen permutations of results from the final three games affecting the title race, but popular opinion was that both Ipswich and Burnley would win on the Saturday, meaning the title would be decided at Hillsborough on the Monday. Ipswich and Burnley officials arranged to supply each other with fifteen-minute updates by telephone of the scorelines at the two Saturday games.

Town players were naturally optimistic that the title was coming to Suffolk and scoffed at the pundits who still harboured doubts. Skipper Nelson said: 'I find it astounding that despite the fact that we have lost only twelve of 51 League and cup games we are still regarded as very much the country cousins by the grudging sporting press. Some of the writers must by now be asking if Ipswich are as bad as they first thought.

Supporter John Plummer of Clacton was fifteen at the time and recalled that, bizarrely, a group of Spurs mascots turned up for the Villa game, and paraded around the pitch in full regalia, displaying a banner that read: 'Spurs fans wish the Town the best of luck.' John believes Spurs followers were very keen that the title they currently held should remain in the south and not disappear to Lancashire. As the banner made its way past the Churchman's End, the home crowd spontaneously broke into Tottenham's 'glory, glory' anthem to acknowledge the gesture.

Villa came to Suffolk free from any pressure to get a result, but manager Joe Mercer promised they would give 100 percent effort. Ipswich hoped the same would go for Burnley's opponents, Chelsea.

John Elsworthy recalls: 'We were very tentative that day against Villa. I stayed back mostly and we were a bit frightened about making a mistake and didn't look like scoring for 70 minutes. Then I raced into the box for Roy Stephenson's free-kick. It was a beautiful ball which I met with my head but could see straight away it was going to hit the bar.' To everyone's relief Crawford anticipated this too, and was on hand to dive forward and nod home the rebound. Relief and unbounded joy all round. As the *EADT* later reported: 'Staid respectable businessmen threw their hats off, never caring if they ever saw them again, small boys squeaked and squealed and all was joy indeed!'

The Midlanders' response to the pandemonium was bold. They threw men forward in search of an equaliser. It meant Town would get the chance to net a second if they could break quickly against the under-manned Villa defence. When the ball was hooked out of Town's box on 76 minutes, only Villa's John Sleeuwenhoek and Crawford were up near the halfway line to fight for it. The Town centre-forward – roared on by his adoring fans – got clear of his marker and headed goalwards. Goalkeeper Nigel Sims advanced and got a hand to the ball, appearing for a second to have averted the danger. But Crawford kept his balance, adjusted his position and stretched to hook the loose ball viciously home. At 2-0, that really was that, and now Villa's resistance crumbled. Town hit the net twice more in the closing minutes only to be foiled both times by a linesman's raised offside flag.

Midway through the second half, news had spread around the ground that Burnley were being held 1-1, but when the final whistle sounded at Portman Road, the final score from Turf Moor hadn't been established. Town fans invaded the pitch in celebration anyway. The players battled to get off, unaware whether or not they were champions. Crawford and Leadbetter failed to reach the tunnel before being hoisted shoulder-high. It took several minutes of confusion before a broad Suffolk accent was heard on the tannoy confirming that Burnley had only drawn and Town were therefore champions. An almighty roar went up and the players and officials came out to join in the fun. Those that had reached the dressing rooms soon returned, including a shirtless Billy Baxter, sipping what looked like lemonade. Crawford was still being paraded on the shoulders of two fans, one of whom was the immaculately dressed Jim Crane from Haughley. It was a moment captured by press photographers and one that Jim, wearing his trademark blue suit and dicky bow, loves to recall: 'I'll never forget it as long as I live. At the whistle everyone ran on and I went straight from the Churchman's Stand and headed for Crawford and hoisted him up on my shoulder. A lot was made later of the press pictures of me in my suit, white shirt and dicky bow, but I always dressed like this for games. It was a blue suit and I was just sporting the colours. I remember getting home later and going to my parents' house where I saw a clip on Anglia TV news which showed me on the field holding Crawford up. I got on my moped and drove round the village scream-ing that we were champions. It was a fantastic day and many of us ended up in the King's Arms in Haughley where we had a great night, singing and drinking till about 5 in the morning.'

Another fan who spotted himself in press photos of the pitch invasion was Phil Baldry, then aged eleven. His mum Florence said she and Phil had arrived very early to get their usual place in the Church-man's End: 'Little Phil was allowed down the front where he was lift-ed over the railings and allowed to sit on the grass. After the final whistle the pitch became full of people hugging and kissing – but where on earth was Phil? He was so excited when he finally did show up – he'd actually touched Ray Crawford's foot!' Florence says she always wore a smart coat and high heels to matches in those days, but 40 years later at the age of 81 she prefers a replica Town shirt and trainers. Phil died in 2001 and the club agreed to allow his ashes to be buried close to the spot from where Crawford headed the vital first goal against Villa.

Another pitch-invading young fan was ten-year-old Dave Allard from Stonham Parva, who later became a journalist. In 2002 he had completed nearly 25 years covering Town matches. 'I was one of the fans who flooded on the pitch and I followed as the bigger lads chaired off goalkeeper Bailey. Back in Stonham that night, on a local field, my mates and I played out the game again. Glamour boy Crawford was my biggest hero and I had to be him. But I'd been with the brigade who carried Bailey off and I had to dive around and be him as well.' Meanwhile, Bryan Barker of Ipswich recalls that after the game he went out dancing in Norwich with his girlfriend and found that even in enemy territory the place was decked out in blue and white favours.

While the fans and players celebrated on the pitch, behind the stands Cliff Michelmore of the BBC was interviewing a beaming Chairman Cobbold and handing over the six bottles of champagne that his colleague Kenneth Wolstenholme had promised if Town finished above Spurs. There was no sign of *Daily Express* reporter Desmond Hackett, who'd promised to eat his hat if Town won the title. A slightly breathless, but relatively composed Alf Ramsey told reporters there could never be another season like this for Ipswich, unless they won the European Cup the following year. 'I've been lucky to get no serious injuries,' he said. 'We did well because we practice, practice and practice. All weaknesses – the opposition's and ours – are examined and discussed.' His wife Vickie said her man would soon be having an extended three-week holiday in Spain after such a hectic season.

In the dressing rooms the champagne and Tolly bottled beer soon began to flow. Trainer Jimmy Forsyth voluntarily jumped into the communal bath fully clothed, having earlier heard that the players were planning to throw him in anyway. Amidst all the fun and games, few noticed the arrival of the fire brigade to deal with a small fire which broke out at the Churchman's End. Telegrams and congratulatory phone calls rained into the club office. Burnley chairman Bob Lord got through by phone, while John Elsworthy had telegrams from his former commanding officer Vice-Admiral Hesketh, and motorcycle champion Dave Bickers, a relative of his wife.

Although celebrations at the ground were long and loud, there was no trophy to be paraded as the League had evidently not expected a definite outcome until the following Monday. There was also no victory parade in Ipswich that weekend as Town were leaving on a continental tour, meaning the celebratory parties would have to wait. Less than two hours after the end of the match, the ground played host to the Saul Charity Cup final between local sides Ranelagh Road and Melton United. Refereeing this game was Geoff Lord, who recalled: 'Our dressing room was the size of a broom cupboard but we could see the empty champagne bottles lying around the floor in the main dressing rooms. John Cobbold came in and wished us all the best with a glass of champagne in his hand – he didn't offer us one though!'

After the initial jubilation died down, commentators and reporters attempted to put in perspective what Town had achieved. No other

club had won the title in their first season at top level. Five players –
Bailey, Carberry, Elsworthy, Phillips and Leadbetter – had become the
only players to have won First, Second and Third Division championship medals with the same club. Elsworthy went one better, as he
had an additional Third Division medal from 1953. The three divi-
sional titles had been won by Ipswich within a period of just six years
– far quicker than by Wolves and Derby, who by 2002 were the only
other clubs to have won all three. Graham Taylor of the *Sporting Life*
wrote: 'Had Ipswich won the title two or three seasons ago it would
have been shrugged off as one of those things. But what astonishes
critics and supporters alike is that the Suffolk club has pulled off the
impossible at a time when everything is now against the poor clubs
doing well.'

Fan Steve Prentice says: 'It all unfolded like a wonderful dream and
I'm sure that no supporters actually believed we could win the championship until after Burnley inexplicably slipped up.' Burnley's late-
season collapse was indeed a major factor, as was the inability of Spurs
to mount a serious challenge after Christmas. Burnley centre-half
Tommy Cummings said it was a 'true tragedy' that his side tossed away
the title. In the book, *Burnley: The Glory Years*, he suggested that certain
team-mates didn't pull their weight in the League after reaching the
Cup final (which they subsequently lost): 'I wasn't a player to shirk
tackles, but there must have been others where it did happen.'

In the cold light of day, even Town fans were willing to accept that
Town enjoyed a decent amount of luck in 1961-62. Elvin King, another fan who later became a sports writer, says: 'To be honest it was not
a particularly strong season in Division One. There were a number of
weak teams, and Town probably lost more games than most other
champions over the years. I'm not saying they were lucky – for they
were magnificently managed. They were round pegs in round holes,
playing to a unique plan that baffled the rest for enough time for the
title to be won. The players can consider themselves lucky as few, if
any, had the talent to have found fame elsewhere. They were basically
journeymen Second and Third Division players until Ramsey instilled
his magic. It was the system rather than ability that did it, although
Crawford does remain Town's best ever natural finisher and he and
Phillips worked very well in tandem. I feel Baxter was the most talented by some distance. Carberry and Compton were ordinary and so

was keeper Bailey and Nelson. Elsworthy did have grace and an eye for the telling pass but certainly no pace or strength. Stephenson was average with a good crossing foot, while Moran was little more than a forager who had half an eye for goal. Leadbetter had no pace or strength whatsoever and would have been wiped out within seconds in the modern game. However, he probably contributed more than anybody because he found so much space and created so many chances with astute balls into the box. Becoming champions was the type of romantic event that will never happen again.'

The Suffolk journeymen who had now qualified for the European Cup were taking home around £25 per week each at this time. They shared £1,500 'talent money' from the club as a one-off reward, and over the course of the 1961-62 season had shared £1,344 in bonuses. They were not rich men, but their achievement won them unprecedented recognition for sportsmen from eastern England. Less than 48 hours after the Villa game they departed for a four-game tour of the Continent. Hundreds of fellow passengers on the ferry bound for the Hook of Holland applauded as they boarded at Harwich. Also awaiting them was a box of Australian apples, sent to the quayside by the people of Ipswich in Queensland, a town formed by East Anglian settlers 100 years earlier. During the trip, which featured two wins and two defeats against German and Danish sides, Town were feted as champions of England and on one occasion introduced as guests of honour to a 70,000 crowd at a big German domestic game.

Only sixteen players had been called upon to win the League title (eleven of whom made 37 appearances or more), but all 28 players on the club's books were retained for the following season. After returning from their European tour, the trophy was finally handed over and paraded around Ipswich prior to a civic reception on the Cornhill. An estimated 10,000-plus squeezed into the town centre and a surging mass in Tavern Street at one point pushed police back 50 yards before order was restored. The team and its open-topped bus was preceded by the band of the Royal Marines from nearby Shotley. At a subsequent banquet at the Manor House, supporters' club chairman Stanley Butler called Ramsey the best manager in the world, who had been a 'Christopher Columbus' as far as Ipswich was concerned.

John Cobbold and the directors later held a lavish banquet at London's Savoy Hotel and nearly all the other League clubs sent representatives. Bob Lord told the gathering that if his beloved Burnley had to fail, he was glad it had been Ipswich who'd triumphed, but he couldn't resist saying that he believed his men had thrown the title away. 'Given the run of the ball, in twelve months you will win the European Cup,' he predicted. Afterwards, the championship trophy was entrusted for a while to skipper Nelson, who took it home with him. He recalls his children having fun taking photos of it in the back garden, before dad tucked it away for safe keeping in a cupboard. An unreal ending to an unreal season.

Alf Ramsey, John Cobbold and keeper Roy Bailey celebrate in the Mayor's Parlour (May 1962)

Skipper Andy Nelson says a few words in the Mayor's Parlour

Ted Phillips picks up another, Roy Bailey says 'cheers', while Ray Crawford has had one too many!

The players acknowledge the cheering crowds on the steps of the Town Hall (May 1962)

John Elsworthy (left) and trainer Jimmy Forsyth show the trophy to the cheering crowds below

Andy Nelson holds up the trophy, Roy Bailey has a hold of its base, and the band plays on

Police struggle to hold back the crowd in Tavern Street during the victory parade (May 1962)

Chapter Nine

~ *How the Mighty Fell* ~

Post-1962

Less than eighteen months after becoming champions of England, Ipswich Town was a club in crisis. Rock bottom of Division One, the established stars were well past their best, new signings were not up to the job, and the new manager – Ramsey's successor – was out of his depth. Attendances slumped and there was no money to buy new talent. On the way to inevitable relegation, Town conceded ten goals in a single match at Fulham, nine at Stoke, seven to Manchester United and were thrashed 0-6 on three separate occasions. To make matters worse, the club's squeaky clean image was tarnished by some players' behaviour off the field. Rarely, if ever, can the Champions of England have been brought to earth so quickly or so brutally.

In fact, Town were on the slippery slope from the very first competitive match after winning the title in April 1962. The Charity Shield contest against FA Cup winners Spurs – a traditional curtain raiser in the August sunshine – saw Town hammered 1-5 at Portman Road. Spurs boss Bill Nicholson had by now worked out how to combat Town's system. His wing-halves marked Town's deep-lying wingers and he tucked his full-backs inside, alongside the centre-half, to deny Crawford and Phillips space. The strategy worked so well that it broke the spell that Ramsey seemed to enjoy over his opponents. Ipswich would no longer benefit from the element of surprise that had carried them so far, so quickly.

Alf Ramsey, however, believed a title-winning side couldn't possibly be relegated the following year. Admittedly hampered by a lack of funds, he remained unwilling (or unable?) to bolster his ageing squad or to try new tactics. Having achieved the impossible dream, he now seemed fazed by the task of following it. One assumes this inscrutable man knew deep down that his work was done at Ipswich and that new challenges would beckon elsewhere. Moreover, the success he'd achieved at Ipswich was not built on firm foundations: there was no youth policy or scouting network in place. His had been a magnificent achievement but it bore all the hallmarks of being a complete one-off.

His loyalty to his players was a recognised and lauded trait, but with hindsight it seems short-sighted to have retained all 28 players on the staff, for the squad was clearly too old and full of dead wood. Eight of the championship-winning side were 30 or over and just one was under 25. Yet despite this, the only new face to arrive in the summer of 1962 was Bobby Blackwood of Hearts, who was almost 28.

In addition, there was clearly unrest in the camp even before 1962-63 kicked off. Ray Crawford and Billy Baxter held out for more money. Both eventually re-signed, but Crawford thought he deserved more than £30 per week and had a transfer request denied. Town's start was bad enough – two wins from the first seven games – but it was followed by a run of nine League games without a win. The defence looked shaky and Bailey made a series of costly errors in goal. Despite his advancing years, Jimmy Leadbetter was still in the side and he even hit a hat-trick in the FA Cup against Mansfield. Leadbetter's famously senior-citizen appearance had always been a source of hilarity to his colleagues and after his hat-trick goal they comically picked him up and carried him gently back to his own half to save his legs. On another occasion, he was wheeled through an airport terminal in a wheelchair by team-mate Blackwood.

During an unhappy autumn, Birmingham came to Portman Road and won 5-1, thanks to a slipshod display by the defence. From Ipswich's point of view, further bad news arrived on 25 October 1962 when it was announced that Ramsey would succeed Walter Winterbottom as England manager. It was rumoured that Jimmy Adamson had turned down the job, and it had taken Ramsey around a month to decide to accept it. He did, however, also agree to stay at Ipswich for a limited period, to steer them through a difficult season and help his successor settle in. This meant Ramsey would be a part-time employee at the FA for the first six months. At the time, this seemed a gentlemanly thing to do, so far as Ipswich were concerned, but maybe his presence merely served to postpone the essential major surgery that the team so desperately needed. Town embarked on their European Cup debut while seeking only their third manager since they joined the League 24 years earlier. Jimmy Dickinson of Portsmouth was touted by the press as a leading candidate.

The only real pre-Christmas excitement for the fans came in the European Cup, when a woefully weak Floriana of Malta were beaten

10-0 at Portman Road, Crawford netting five. The away leg, played on a grassless dustbowl of a pitch, had already seen a 4-1 Town victory. AC Milan posed a rather more serious threat in the next round and, in front of a nearly empty San Siro Stadium, Town lost 0-3. The players complained about previously unheard-of gamesmanship by the Italian side, not to mention the 'blinding' of keeper Bailey by dozens of flash photographs at set-pieces. Ipswich's battling 2-1 win in the second leg proved to be easily their best performance of the entire season, and they were unlucky not to score more. Crawford recalls nearly missing this game after his new car broke down on the Norwich Road, leaving him stranded with kick-off time looming. 'I eventually got a lift to the ground but Alf just said: "Come on Ray it's getting a bit late – fifteen minutes to kick-off".'

Town slumped into the depths of Division One and by December relegation looked a strong possibility. Even a rare victory – 2-0 over Sheffield Wednesday – would later be tainted. *The People* sensationally alleged that the match had been fixed. It emerged that three Wednesday players – David 'Bronco' Layne, Peter Swan and Tony Kay – placed £50 each on a fixed-odds bet which would pay rich dividends if they lost at Ipswich, and if York and Lincoln won other games. The resulting scandal and court case led to Layne and Swan being jailed and all three were banned from playing for life. Contemporary match reports of the Ipswich game confirm that Layne and Swan performed badly, but Kay – a youngster set for a long England career – apparently played well. The scandal finished their careers, rocked English soccer, and years later inspired a BBC dramatisation starring Steve Coogan and Michael Elphick.

When Wolves and England half-back Bill Slater, 35, turned down an approach to be the Town's new manager, Chairman Cobbold eventually had to reverse his decision not to advertise the post for fear of attracting letters from 'cranks'. After sifting through 60 applications, only Reg Flewin and Jackie Milburn, managers of Stockport and Yiewsley respectively, were deemed worthy of interview. Milburn was grilled in the morning and told to return later in the day for the verdict. The former Newcastle centre-forward spent the afternoon 'brooding' in a local cinema, while his wife, clearly more confident, visited the town's estate agents. It was a close run thing, but Milburn got the nod.

Milburn would later recall that he phoned Ramsey before applying and was warned that Ipswich had little strength in depth and precious little money, so he did have an idea what he was taking on. He started work in January 1963, but would not get full control until 29 April, when Ramsey finally departed. In coming to Ipswich, Milburn called a halt to his own playing career, which was a disappointment for Southern League Yiewsley (later renamed Hillingdon Borough) where he'd been an enthusiastic player-manager for two years. Prior to this, he'd been in Northern Ireland for three years as player-manager of Linfield, for whom he had played in the European Cup and scored over a ton of goals. 'Wor Jackie', now 38, was a cousin of the Charlton brothers, and a former pro sprinter with the appropriate initials 'JET'. He'd made his name in the 1950s at Newcastle where he was a true folk hero. For some England games he'd roomed with Ramsey.

Shortly after his arrival, Milburn joined Ramsey and the Ipswich players on the training pitch and in his first practice match was clobbered by a fierce Ramsey tackle. Initially baffled, the new man would later ruefully recall that the last time they'd met on the field he'd retaliated after a bad foul by pushing Ramsey to the ground, even though it wasn't Alf who had fouled him. Then, Ramsey had not reacted, but now, eight years later, Milburn got his belated come-uppance!

Milburn saw Ipswich in action for the first time at Leicester – a dismal performance that brought a 0-3 defeat, and it ought to have been worse. Leaving Filbert Street with Ramsey, Milburn is said to have been spotted by an old friend who jokingly called out: 'For God's sake, resign immediately.' Milburn recalled Town looking hopeless that day, yet Ramsey, sitting alongside him, astonished him by continuing to insist that Town could win, even after Leicester went three up. Noting the lack of a youth scheme or scouting system, Milburn soon realised Ipswich was a First Division club with a Fourth Division set-up.

With the big freeze of 1962-63 playing havoc with the fixture list, Milburn had time to familiarise himself with the players and the club, while Ramsey remained in overall command and divided his attention between club and country. Ex-Ipswich player Brian Siddall, now an estate agent, helped Milburn find a house. The mild-mannered Geordie steeled himself for the task ahead. It was not an easy time: one journalist recalled seeing him sitting alone in a corner after a game, calming his nerves by doing a crossword.

Throughout March, as Town ploughed through their backlog of fixtures, relegation remained a threat. In addition to below-par displays, the side was disrupted by the type of niggly injuries that they had been free of during their championship year. Keeper Bailey regularly dropped clangers and his replacement, Wilf Hall, was also out of luck at West Brom, going off injured as the side tumbled 1-6. That was merely the worst result in a run of six defeats and a draw, which saw 24 goals conceded. With Ramsey preparing to depart and Milburn unable to make firm decisions, the situation was deteriorating and was made worse by the lack of desperately needed signings. Inevitably, something had to give, and cosy Portman Road was hit by a rare event – a split in the boardroom. Director Ernest Steel resigned after fifteen years' service, declaring that Ramsey and the directors had been negligent in not signing new players to stop the rot. He called fellow directors a bunch of Ramsey 'yes men'. 'Time after time I begged the others to face reality and strengthen the side, but they always said let's leave that to Mr Ramsey, shall we?' Tony Garnett of the *EADT* wrote: 'It is distasteful in the extreme that after the phenomenal success of last year, we should now find ourselves criticising Mr Ramsey, but that is in effect what Mr Steel is doing and there is no gainsaying that he has made out a pretty good case.'

To make matters worse, chairman Cobbold promised to respond to the row with a public statement – but never delivered. Many fans agreed with Steel and demanded explanations from the board, but the best Cobbold could come up with was: 'So much has been said already that the board will make no comment on the matter.' This seemed like a monumental PR blunder, but the affable chairman got away with it, largely because Town won their next two matches – against Sheffield Wednesday and Burnley – and gave themselves a chance of escaping the drop. The winner against Burnley came from the boot of Phillips and was so powerfully struck that it literally broke the net. It had probably been no coincidence that the improved results of April 1963 were achieved after the championship-winning XI took the field together for the first time in nearly twelve months.

With the season having to extend well into May, it needed a draw at Wolves and a surprisingly comfortable 4-1 Friday night win over Bolton to stave off relegation alongside the division's whipping boys Leyton Orient. These two life-saving results were achieved in the fortnight following Ramsey's departure and gave cause to believe that 'Mr Nice Guy' Milburn might do well in his new role. The players and staff had presented Ramsey with an automatic tea-maker as a farewell gift, and the England boss responded in optimistic fashion by saying he was sure Town would go from strength to strength. Milburn must have privately questioned this sentiment, for he'd been left with the task of completely rebuilding the squad with little raw material readily available. To help him scour the UK for talent, trainer Jimmy Forsyth's brother was given the task of scouting in Scotland. Milburn made many trips north of the border to inspect his findings. Within a month or two he'd chased up dozens of leads and had recruited John Colrain (Clyde), Jim Thorburn and Jack Bolton (both Raith), Joe Davin (Hibs), Danny Hegan and Jimmy Nelson (both Sunderland) and Joe Broadfoot (Millwall). Only Broadfoot and Hegan would ultimately prove good buys.

Hegan was a highly skilled forward and a real character. Former 'A' team man Mick Banthorpe recalls: 'I was conducting training sessions with a local junior side and asked Danny if he would come and help out on Wednesday nights. He agreed and these sessions always turned into lengthy visits to a lively social club afterwards. I often wondered how Danny, a married man, got away with this. Then one day Danny's wife Patsy asked me to tell my dad not to keep Danny talking so late every Wednesday night. Apparently the maestro Hegan had told Patsy that every Wednesday he spent hours talking football to my dad over a mug of cocoa. Danny had a great sense of humour and used to talk of his time at Albion Rovers, when the crowds were so small they used to announce the crowd changes to the players.'

To finance the influx of new men, Milburn had to sell Town's terrace hero Crawford to Wolves for £42,000. This happened shortly after the Great Train Robbery, but many Town fans considered the Crawford deal an even bigger steal. Crawford explained: 'I didn't ask to leave, but Jackie needed the money and probably thought I was the only one he could sell. At home one evening I was bathing my baby and there was a knock at the door. It was the legendary Stan Cullis of Wolves, and I'd opened the door in an apron.'

John Elsworthy says: 'Jackie was the nicest bloke you could wish to meet, but things generally went badly for him. Two seasons like our title-winning years really takes a lot out of players and you simply can't afford to relax in the aftermath. The club was going downhill and Jackie's Scottish signings only seemed to accelerate the slide.' Billy Baxter, a Scot himself, confirmed this: 'Perhaps Milburn's biggest mistake was getting too many Scots together, for they started drinking and misbehaving and he couldn't do anything with them.' Tony Garnett recalled an occasion when two players slipped out of the team's hotel without permission on the night before a match at Birmingham. 'Milburn couldn't believe it. He was close to tears and at a loss to know what sort of disciplinary action to take.'

Things went from bad to worse as the 1963-64 season unfolded. After beating Burnley on the season's opening day, Town slumped to the bottom of the table by 1 October and would never recover. A run of 23 games without a win included a 2-7 home defeat by Manchester United and 0-6 maulings at Bolton and Arsenal, with a League Cup defeat at lowly Third Division Walsall thrown in for good measure. Three penalties were awarded to Town during the campaign and all three were missed. Attendances plummeted and relegation looked a certainty well before Christmas. It took many weeks to find a replacement for Crawford and even skipper Andy Nelson was dropped in November. The big centre-half immediately asked for his column in the local paper to be discontinued as it would be an 'embarrassment' in the circumstances.

Everyone of a certain age recalls where they were when they heard of President Kennedy's assassination. Town's players were preparing for the next day's home match with Spurs. For the match, the players wore black armbands and observed a minute's silence before Bill Nicholson's men won 3-2. Things then hit a new low on Boxing Day 1963. Ten First Division matches produced an astonishing 66 goals – and ten of them went into Ipswich's net. A club record defeat, 1-10 by modest Fulham, included one goal from Bobby Robson and a hattrick achieved in a record-breaking 210 seconds by Graham Leggat. The tenth goal summed up Town's day, Leggat's last-minute cross sailing straight into the net through the fog. Milburn put on a brave face and said the game had been a one-off: 'We must stick to our plan. I hope we have learned something. We must not play football at walking pace. We were at sixes and sevens.' Such a result in today's game would cause heads to roll, but the board stayed true to Milburn and only one team change was made for the next match.

Milburn's faith was rewarded two days later when Town turned the tables and beat Fulham 4-2 in the Portman Road return. This, the third win of the season, raised a flicker of hope, as did the encouraging form of new signing Gerry Baker, who bagged eight goals in his first nine games. In the New Year, American-born Baker rewarded himself with a car, the first new one he'd bought, after getting through seventeen second-hand models in two years. The spectre of relegation was forgotten briefly during January's FA Cup home tie with Stoke, for it brought Stanley Matthews to Portman Road. Matthews was still playing, and he would shortly turn 49. Suddenly the Town side looked young again.

Town's away form in 1963-64 was abysmal. They failed to win a game on their travels, including two trips in the cups. The Fulham disaster was almost repeated at Stoke, when the home side gratefully accepted nine goals. Their ninth made it 100 conceded by Ipswich in the League, even though eight more games remained. The *EADT* described Town's display as 'putrid'. New keeper Thorburn had only just broken into the first team after a long wait in the reserves and 'A' teams, but the nine goals at Stoke came in the wake of six conceded at Liverpool, which meant he was inevitably left out again. The returning Bailey also looked ill at ease, but when poor Thorburn was recalled he promptly let in another six at Tottenham. Supporters raised the question of why Milburn had signed a goalkeeper who'd let in 114 during the previous season at Raith. The misery by now was relentless, and the *EADT* commented: 'The team's approach to the game is at times pitifully casual and lacking in any sort of pluck or zest. Too many times, usually away from home, Ipswich have just gone through the motions.'

After the Stoke debacle, stories in the national press alleged Town players had been involved in an unsavoury fracas at a jazz club and at the supporters' club, and that they often indulged in bad language and heavy drinking in local pubs. Poor Milburn, not knowing which way to turn, agreed the name of the club was being dragged through the mud and offered to resign if that was what the fans wanted. Few held him personally responsible, however, and he somehow survived. He later recalled how he spent hours during this period brooding in a darkened room, took to drinking gin like it was going out of fashion, and suffered grotesque swellings on his face due to all the stress.

Relegation was finally confirmed on 11 April 1964, the day Town happened to beat Aston Villa 4-3 in front of a Portman Road crowd of under 12,000. Bizarrely, this was one of three 4-3 victories over the closing weeks, but depressingly it was one of ten home games when the attendance fell below the 15,000 mark. It was only the club's second relegation in its history, but it had been inevitable for several months. The season ended with a 4-3 win over ten-man Blackpool, the goals conceded taking the season's tally to an horrific 121. But once again there was no wholesale summer clearout and just four men were released. One of these was long-serving keeper Bailey, who'd had a dreadful season by his standards, but, curiously, the club did a U-turn later in the summer and re-engaged him.

Milburn's first season had frankly been disastrous, but to his credit he ploughed on tirelessly, covering thousands of miles by car, rail and air to seek out new talent. His pair of signings in the summer of 1964 – winger Frank Brogan from Celtic and full-back Mick McNeil from Middlesbrough – both proved excellent investments, which cannot be said for most of his earlier recruits.

As 1964-65 got under way in the Second Division, the club was still in turmoil behind the scenes. Nelson and Phillips were on the transfer list, and an unhappy Baxter joined them for a spell. Broadfoot also considered quitting the game to make use of his recently acquired London cabbie's licence. Remarkably, that grand old survivor Leadbetter was still on the books, and commenced his ninth season in the team, aged 36. Town looked an unhappy bunch and things predictably got off to a bad start. The first two home matches ended in defeats by Coventry and Preston, the latter by an embarrassing 1-5 margin. The writing was on the wall for Milburn, and shortly after a 3-5 defeat in the return with Coventry, he quit. The chairman tried to change his mind, but the clinching factor was Milburn's health, which was beginning to suffer badly on account of the club's continuing downward spiral.

Trainer Forsyth was put in temporary charge as tributes were paid to Milburn for his hard work, unfailing courtesy and his integrity in turning down tabloid offers to 'blow the lid off Ipswich'. Many agreed he was 'too nice' to be a top manager, although he deserved credit for putting in place a youth policy and scouting network that would greatly benefit the club in later years. After the gentlemanly approach

adopted by Milburn, perhaps Town now needed to employ a discipli-
narian, someone with a ruthless streak who could turn the club upside
down and start afresh. In October 1964 Bill McGarry arrived and
proved to be just that man.

By the late spring of 1965 – just 36 months on – only one of the
seventeen-man championship-winning squad remained at Portman
Road. This was Billy Baxter, who would go on to skipper Town to
another Second Division title in 1968, before moving to Hull in 1971.
He departed on bad terms with manager Bobby Robson and did not
return to Suffolk until a players' reunion 31 years later. In 1997 he
needed all his legendary toughness and courage to cope with a leg
amputation. 'This was not due to football,' he explained, 'but because
I'm diabetic and have bad circulation. It happened and I have to get
on with it. I'm not able to drink alcohol any more and I like to keep
fit by going to the gym regularly.'

Whither the other 1962 heroes? Ramsey, of course, went on to
achieve a knighthood and Jules Rimet glory with England, but continued living in Ipswich, purchasing a modest home in Valley Road with
his bonus for winning the World Cup. Concern over Ramsey's health
first emerged when he failed to attend the 1993 memorial service for
Bobby Moore. He made his final public appearance in 1994 when an
Anglia Railways train was named after him. Later his former near-
neighbour Bobby Robson was appalled to hear Ramsey was spending
weeks confined to an NHS hospital ward and spearheaded the fund-
ing of private care. Ramsey subsequently died in 1998 of prostate cancer, with Alzheimer's disease given as a secondary cause. He passed
away in the same week that Town supporters announced plans to erect
a statue in his honour. In 2001, his widow carried out his wish that a
collection of his football memorabilia be auctioned off at Christie's.

Ray Crawford returned to Portman Road in 1966 and spent a further three years leading the attack at his spiritual home. After spells at
Charlton, Kettering and Colchester he returned to his native south
coast to coach at Portsmouth before going into merchandising. Ted
Phillips had brief stints at Leyton Orient, Luton, Colchester and
Floriana (Malta) before cable-laying for British Telecom. He did well
in club cricket and became a regular spectator on the Portman Road
terraces. John Elsworthy quit football in 1964 after McGarry's arrival
and ran a grocery store and then a post office before retiring in 1993.

He became chairman of the club's development association. Jimmy Leadbetter left Town in 1965 and became Sudbury Town player-manager until 1973. After spells as a newsagent and salesman, he returned to his native Edinburgh and worked as a driver before retiring in 1993. Roy Bailey left Town in 1964 for South Africa, where he became national coach and a TV commentator. He died after illness in 1993. Larry Carberry left in 1965 to play for Barrow and settled on his native Merseyside where he became a docker for nineteen years until made redundant in 1989. John Compton signed for Bournemouth in 1964 and after hanging up his boots became a tanker driver in Poole. Andy Nelson joined Leyton Orient in 1964 and had two seasons with Plymouth before becoming a coach at Millwall and then manager of Gillingham in 1971. He managed Charlton between 1974 and 1979 before taking charge of their commercial department, later emigrating to Spain. Roy Stephenson played for local non-league sides after leaving Town in 1965 and was a salesman until retirement in 1996. He died in 2000 from stomach cancer. Doug Moran left Suffolk in 1964 to play for Dundee United and Falkirk and then spent around 30 years as a pensions adviser in Edinburgh.

Following his horrendous experience in soccer management, Jackie Milburn switched to a career in football journalism, based in Newcastle. Given a belated testimonial at St James' Park, an astonishing crowd of 45,404 welcomed him home. He died of cancer in 1988 and the city was brought to a virtual standstill by his funeral.

Mascots 'Swede' Herring and young Ian Harvey entertain the crowd before Ipswich's first European home tie, against Floriana of Malta, which they won 10-0 (September 1962)

Alf Ramsey is the centre of attention, but not to the two giggling ladies on the right

Mascots 'Swede' Herring (a bus conductor), 'Miss Switch' (Glenys Hayward) and young Ian Harvey

Doug Moran (left) is tracked by West Brom's Don Howe (September 1963)

Ted Phillips' close-range shot is saved by Chelsea keeper Bonetti in a 1-3 defeat (October 1963)

~ *Guide to Seasonal Summaries* ~

Col 1:   Match number (for league fixtures); Round (for cup-ties).
         e.g. 2:1 means 'Second round; first leg'.
         e.g. 4R means 'Fourth round replay'.

Col 2:   Date of the fixture and whether Home (H), Away (A), or Neutral (N).

Col 3:   Opposition.

Col 4:   Attendances. Home gates appear in roman; Away gates in *italics*.
         Figures in **bold** indicate the largest and smallest, at home and away.
         Average home and away attendances appear after the final league match.

Col 5:   Respective league positions of Ipswich and their opponents after the match.
         Ipswich's position appears on the top line in roman.
         Their opponents' position appears on the second line in *italics*.
         For cup-ties, the division and position of opponents is provided.
         e.g. 2:12 means the opposition are twelfth in Division 2.

Col 6:   The top line shows the result: W(in), D(raw), or L(ose).
         The second line shows Ipswich's cumulative points total.

Col 7:   The match score, Ipswich's given first.
         Scores in bold indicate Ipswich's biggest league win and heaviest defeat.

Col 8:   The half-time score, Ipswich's given first.

Col 9:   The top line shows Ipswich's scorers and times of goals in roman.
         The second line shows opponents' scorers and times of goals in *italics*.
         A 'p' after the time of a goal denotes a penalty; 'og' an own-goal.
         The third line gives the name of the match referee.

Team line-ups: Ipswich line-ups appear on the top line, irrespective of whether
         they are home or away. Opposition teams appear on the second line in *italics*.
         Players of either side who are sent off are marked !
         Ipswich players making their league debuts are displayed in **bold**.

N.B.   For clarity, all information appearing in *italics* relates to opposing teams.

LEAGUE DIVISION 2 — Manager: Alf Ramsey — SEASON 1960-61

1. (A) 20/8 LEYTON ORIENT — W 3-1 (H-T 2-0) | Att 14,798 | Pos 2 | Pt 2
Scorers, Times: Rees 25, 37, Crawford 90 / Johnston 51
Ref: D Howell

	1	2	3	4	5	6	7	8	9	10	11
Ipswich	Bailey	Carberry	Malcolm	Pickett	Nelson	Elsworthy	Siddall	Rees	Crawford	Phillips	Leadbetter
Leyton Orient	George	Eagles	Lewis	Facey	Bishop	Sowell	White	Foster	Johnston	Graham	McDonald

Bailey has a fine game on his return from knee surgery. Rees converts a loose ball after Phillips' shot is parried. Frank George flaps at Malcolm's cross and Rees nods in. Bailey catches a cross but Johnston barges him and the ball over the line. Crawford heads in a late clincher.

2. (A) 25/8 SCUNTHORPE — L 0-4 (H-T 0-4) | Att 11,130 | Pt 2
Scorers, Times: Marriott 17, Godfrey 37, Neale 39, [Thomas 43]
Ref: K Collinge

	1	2	3	4	5	6	7	8	9	10	11
Ipswich	Bailey	Carberry	Malcolm	Pickett	Nelson	Elsworthy	Siddall	Rees	Crawford	Phillips	Leadbetter
Scunthorpe	Jones	John	Brownsword	Gibson	Heward	Neale	Marriott	Godfrey	Thomas	Bonson	Bakes

Ramsey is hopping mad after this Thursday debacle and promises changes. Jack Marriott converts Martin Bakes' cross. Pete Neale clouts a 20-yarder which crosses the line via Bailey and the bar. Barrie Thomas survives a handball appeal to net the third goal in a hectic six-minute spell.

3. (H) 27/8 DERBY — W 4-1 (H-T 1-1) | Att 12,309 | Pt 4
Scorers, Times: Owen 31, Crawford 63, Rees 71, [Elsworthy 78] / Parry 29
Ref: C Woan

	1	2	3	4	5	6	7	8	9	10	11
Ipswich	Hall	Carberry	Malcolm	Pickett	Nelson	Elsworthy	Owen	Rees	Crawford	Phillips	Leadbetter
Derby	Oxford	Barrowcliffe	Conwell	Upton	Young	Davies	Swallow	Parry	Thompson	Darwin	Fagan

Slack defending allows Jack Parry to beat debutant keeper Hall. Two minutes later Ken Oxford collides with a post and breaks his jaw in a vain effort to keep out Owen's intended cross. Parry goes in goal but is beaten by fine headers by Crawford and Rees, and a low Elsworthy drive.

4. (H) 30/8 SCUNTHORPE — W 2-0 (H-T 1-0) | Att 12,426 | Pos 5 | Pt 6
Scorers, Times: Crawford 6, 79
Ref: A Moore

	1	2	3	4	5	6	7	8	9	10	11
Ipswich	Hall	Carberry	Malcolm	Pickett	Nelson	Elsworthy	Owen	Rees	Crawford	Phillips	Leadbetter
Scunthorpe	Jones	John	Brownsword	Gibson	Heward	Neale	Marriott	Godfrey	Thomas	Bonson	Bakes

Elsworthy's through pass sets up Crawford for a vital early breakthrough. Hall, deputising for the unfit Bailey, makes a splendid flying save to prevent new signing Brian Godfrey from equalising. Crawford clinches victory late in this first senior home game to be played on a Tuesday.

5. (A) 3/9 BRISTOL ROV — D 1-1 (H-T 1-1) | Att 15,467 | Pos 4 | Pt 7
Scorers, Times: Phillips 7p / Biggs 44
Ref: W Clements

	1	2	3	4	5	6	7	8	9	10	11
Ipswich	Hall	Carberry	Malcolm	Pickett	Nelson	Elsworthy	Owen	Rees	Crawford	Phillips	Leadbetter
Bristol Rov	Norman	Hillard	Watling	Sykes	Pyle	Mabbutt	Petherbridge	Biggs	Edge	Hamilton	Hooper

David Pyle fouls Crawford and Phillips thunders in the penalty, with Malcolm Norman getting in its path but unable to keep it out. A mediocre encounter comes to life briefly when Alfie Biggs latches on to veteran winger John Watling's cross and the ball bobbles past the flailing Hall.

6. (A) 7/9 BRIGHTON — W 4-2 (H-T 3-2) | Att 12,595 | Pos 3 | Pt 9
Scorers, Times: Crawford 3, 15, 86, Phillips 11 / Laverick 4, Tiddy 30p
Ref: A Sturgeon

	1	2	3	4	5	6	7	8	9	10	11
Ipswich	Hall	Carberry	Malcolm	Pickett	Nelson	Elsworthy	Owen	Rees	Crawford	Phillips	Leadbetter
Brighton	Hollins	McNicholl	Bissett	Bertolini	Jennings	Burtenshaw	Tiddy	McNeill	Thorne	Laverick	Gordon

Leadbetter and Rees set up Crawford's opener. Bobby Laverick heads in an instant response. Phillips thunders in an awesome 25-yarder for one of the best goals of his career. Nelson's handball gives the Seagulls hope, but Crawford completes his hat-trick despite looking offside.

7. (H) 10/9 LIVERPOOL — W 1-0 (H-T 1-0) | Att 13,521 | Pos 2 | Pt 11
Scorers, Times: Phillips 34
Ref: M Fussey

	1	2	3	4	5	6	7	8	9	10	11
Ipswich	Bailey	Carberry	Malcolm	Pickett	Nelson	Elsworthy	Owen	Rees	Crawford	Phillips	Leadbetter
Liverpool	Slater	Molyneux	Moran	Milne	White	Leishman	Lewis	Harrower	Hickson	Melia	Morrissey

Back from injury, Bailey is kept busy and looks sharp. Owen's low cross is laid back and Phillips picks his spot. Jimmy Melia misses two clear chances and Dick White hits a post. As Bill Shankly's men get frustrated, Dave Hickson and Andy Nelson are spoken to after an ugly scuffle.

8. (H) 13/9 BRIGHTON — W 4-0 (H-T 3-0) | Att 14,672 | Pos 1 | Pt 13
Scorers, Times: Phillips 10, 36, Crawford 12, 82
Ref: J. Cooke

	1	2	3	4	5	6	7	8	9	10	11
Ipswich	Bailey	Carberry	Malcolm	Pickett	Nelson	Elsworthy	Owen	Rees	Crawford	Phillips	Leadbetter
Brighton	Hollins	McNicholl	Little	Bertolini	Jennings	Burtenshaw	Tiddy	McNeill	Thorne	Laverick	Curry

Phillips collects a poor goal-kick by Dave Hollins and blasts in. He then carves out a chance for Crawford who drives in the second. The game is beyond Billy Lane's side when Phillips heads in Stephenson's cross. The debutant makes another for Crawford as Town go top of the table.

9. (A) 17/9 ROTHERHAM — D 1-1 (H-T 0-1) | Att 8,873 | Pos 1 | Pt 14
Scorers, Times: Phillips 79 / O'Hara 26
Ref: R Leafe

	1	2	3	4	5	6	7	8	9	10	11
Ipswich	Bailey	Carberry	Malcolm	Pickett	Nelson	Elsworthy	Stephenson	Millward	Crawford	Phillips	Leadbetter
Rotherham	Ironside	Perry	Morgan	Lambert	Madden	Waterhouse	Kirkman	Kettleborough	Sawyer	O'Hara	Bambridge

The table-toppers fail to sparkle at muddy Millmoor. Eddie O'Hara flashes in a fine header. Things improve later and close-passing between Leadbetter and Millward sets up Phillips. Roy Ironside saves from Crawford near the end. New signing Baxter departs to do National Service.

10. (H) 24/9 SOUTHAMPTON — D 3-3 (H-T 1-0) | Att 15,318 | Pos 2 | Pt 15
Scorers, Times: Stephenson 12, Phillips 56, 85 / Paine 52, 60, Mulgrew 82
Ref: J Williams

	1	2	3	4	5	6	7	8	9	10	11
Ipswich	Bailey	Carberry	Malcolm	Pickett	Nelson	Elsworthy	Stephenson	Millward	Crawford	Phillips	Leadbetter
Southampton	Reynolds	Davies	Traynor	Conner	Page	Clifton	Paine	O'Brien	Brown	Mulgrew	Sydenham

In-form Stephenson is on target before Phillips raps a post. Terry Paine bags two equalisers, the second after a Bailey blunder. Tom Mulgrew nets to jeopardise the unbeaten home run. The Churchman's End roars Town forward and Phillips obliges them, equalising with a knee-shot.

Match-by-match record (matches 11–21). Ipswich Town line-up is the upper name in each column; the opponent's player is the italic name beneath.

#	Venue	Opponent	Date	Pos	Res	Score	HT	Att	Opp Pos	Pts
11	A	LEEDS	1/10	2	W	5-2	1:2	13,582	15	17
12	A	CHARLTON	8/10	2	W	2-0	2-0	12,677	11	19
13	H	SHEFFIELD UTD	15/10	2	L	0-1	0-1	19,529	1	19
14	A	STOKE	22/10	2	W	4-2	1:2	8,052	17	21
15	H	SWANSEA	29/10	2	L	0-3	0-2	11,178	19	21
16	A	LUTON	5/11	2	L	2-3	1:1	11,221	19	21
17	H	LINCOLN	12/11	2	W	3-1	0-0	10,197	22	23
18	A	PORTSMOUTH	19/11	3	L	0-1	0-0	11,482	16	23
19	H	HUDDERSFIELD	26/11	3	W	4-2	2-1	11,056	18	25
20	A	SUNDERLAND	3/12	4	L	0-2	0-0	21,251	9	25
21	H	PLYMOUTH	10/12	3	W	3-1	0-1	11,798	8	27

11. LEEDS (A)
Scorers: Crawford 15, 52, 57, Stephenson 48, [Phillips 80] — McCole 7, 40
Ref: C Duxbury
Ipswich: Bailey, Carberry, Malcolm, Pickett, Laurel, Elsworthy, Stephenson, Millward, Crawford, Phillips, Leadbetter
Leeds: Burgin, McGugan, Hair, Cameron, Charlton, Goodwin, Francis, Revie, McCole, Wright, Grainger
John McCole heads in Don Revie's cross and regains the lead for Jack Taylor's men after Crawford levels. After the break Stephenson curls a fine goal and Crawford completes a hat-trick. Ramsey praises a brilliant second-half display but is not so happy about Phillips' transfer request.

12. CHARLTON (A)
Scorers: Phillips 1, Millward 27
Ref: R Mann
Ipswich: Bailey, Carberry, Malcolm, Pickett, Laurel, Elsworthy, Stephenson, Millward, Crawford, Phillips, Leadbetter
Charlton: Duff, Sewell, Townsend, Hinton, Tocknell, Lucas, Lawrie, Edwards, Leary, Werge, Summers
Phillips, having withdrawn his written transfer request, buries a fine header. He's now scored in eight games in a row. Crawford has an effort blocked on the line and Millward tucks in the rebound. It's a fine all-round display by Town and Elsworthy looks a contender for a Wales cap.

13. SHEFFIELD UTD (H)
Scorers: — Russell 4
Ref: R Reddaway
Ipswich: Bailey, Carberry, Malcolm, Pickett, Laurel, Elsworthy, Stephenson, Millward, Crawford, Phillips, Leadbetter
Sheffield Utd: Hodgkinson, Coldwell, Shaw G, Richardson, Shaw J, Summers, Russell, Nibloe, Pace, Hodgson, Simpson
This clash of the table-toppers is a dull affair. Town are out of touch and Johnny Harris's side adopt negative tactics. Acting skipper Malcolm misplaces an early pass and Billy Russell scampers clear to net. Stand-in Laurel has a solid game, subduing Blades' danger-man 'Doc' Pace.

14. STOKE (A)
Scorers: Crawford 43, 52, Phillips 55, [Millward 85] — Bentley 6, Ward D 22
Ref: J McLoughlin
Ipswich: Bailey, Carberry, Malcolm, Pickett, Laurel, Elsworthy, Owen, Millward, Crawford, Phillips, Leadbetter
Stoke: O'Neill, Ward T, Allen, Skeels, Andrew, Asprey, Bentley, Ratcliffe, King, Cairns, Ward D
Tony Bentley's fierce shot and a simple Derek Ward effort shock Town, but Crawford flashes in Leadbetter's through ball at a vital time. Man of the match Owen sets up the equaliser, and moments later Bailey saves Bentley's penalty. Phillips converts Owen's centre as Stoke crumble.

15. SWANSEA (H)
Scorers: — Carberry (og) 28, Williams H 34, [Williams G 59]
Ref: C Rogers
Ipswich: Bailey, Carberry, Malcolm, Pickett, Nelson, Elsworthy, Owen, Millward, Crawford, Phillips, Leadbetter
Swansea: King, Sanders, Griffiths, Hughes, Nurse, Hale, Allchurch, Reynolds, Webster, Williams H, Williams G
Town struggle again at home and Carberry slices a Graham Williams shot past Bailey. With Mel Nurse keeping a tight rein on Crawford and Phillips, Trevor Morris's men go further ahead when Herbie Williams powers clear through the mud. Graham Williams cuts in to shoot a third.

16. LUTON (A)
Scorers: Crawford 30, 87 — Turner 10, 89, Ashworth 47
Ref: E Jennings
Ipswich: Bailey, Carberry, Malcolm, Pickett, Nelson, Elsworthy, Stephenson, Millward, Crawford, Phillips, Leadbetter
Luton: Standen, McNally, Bramwell, Pacey, Groves, McGuffie, Spencer, Ashworth, Turner, Brogan, Tracey
Unmarked Gordon Turner nets for Sam Bartram's side, but Crawford equalises after a Phillips effort hits the bar. Alec Ashworth's low shot restores the home lead, but a late Crawford flick looks to have saved lucky Town. Justice is done when Turner swoops for a dramatic winner.

17. LINCOLN (H)
Scorers: Phillips 52, Millward 54, Crawford 73 — Graver 89
Ref: J Cooke
Ipswich: Bailey, Carberry, Malcolm, Pickett, Nelson, Elsworthy, Stephenson, Millward, Crawford, Phillips, Leadbetter
Lincoln: Heath, Allen, Smith, Middleton, Jackson R, Green, Jackson A, McClelland, Graver, Linnecor, Hawksworth
Against poor opposition, Town struggle in a bleak first half. Blessed relief when Phillips heads in Leadbetter's centre. Confidence restored, moments later Millward stoops to convert Stephenson's cross and the industrious Crawford is rewarded. Graver scrambles a late consolation.

18. PORTSMOUTH (A)
Scorers: — Chapman 70
Ref: A Robottom
Ipswich: Bailey, Carberry, Malcolm, Pickett, Compton, Elsworthy, Stephenson, Millward, Crawford, Phillips, Leadbetter
Portsmouth: Beattie, Rutter, Dickinson, Howells, Gunter, Harris, Priscott, Saunders, White, Chapman, Newman
After a run without a win, Pompey boss Freddie Cox makes changes and his side rally impressively. Only indifferent finishing and fine stops by Bailey keep the score down. Sammy Chapman beats the brave mud-spattered keeper to win the points. Rees nets a hat-trick for the reserves.

19. HUDDERSFIELD (H)
Scorers: Phillips 21p, Millward 41, Crawford 72, [Stephenson 82] — Stokes 10, Low 90
Ref: M Sturgeon
Ipswich: Bailey, Carberry, Malcolm, Pickett, Compton, Elsworthy, Stephenson, Millward, Crawford, Phillips, Leadbetter
Huddersfield: Wood, Parker, Wilson, Taylor, Coddington, Low, McHale, Kerray, Stokes, Massie, McCann
Free-scoring Derek Stokes converts John McCann's pass as Town make another slow start at home. Phillips is brought down and converts himself from the spot. Town go into cruise control and the only hiccup is when defender Gordon Low ventures forward for a consolation goal.

20. SUNDERLAND (A)
Scorers: — McPheat 54, 60
Ref: A Holland
Ipswich: Bailey, Carberry, Malcolm, Pickett, Nelson, Elsworthy, Stephenson, Millward, Crawford, Phillips, Leadbetter
Sunderland: Wakeham, Nelson, Ashurst, Anderson, Hurley, McNab, Hooper, Fagarty, Lawther, McPheat, Overfield
Ramsey is away scouting in Scotland and misses an unhappy occasion as Phillips and Leadbetter both miss good chances early on. Eighteen-year-old Billy McPheat delights the Rokerites and manager Alan Brown with two in six minutes, both fierce drives that give Bailey no chance.

21. PLYMOUTH (H)
Scorers: Crawford 54, 71, Phillips 81 — Kirby 36
Ref: R Jordan
Ipswich: Bailey, Carberry, Malcolm, Pickett, Nelson, Elsworthy, Stephenson, Millward, Crawford, Phillips, Leadbetter
Plymouth: Barnsley, Robertson, Fulton, Williams, Fincham, Newman, Anderson, Carter, Kirby, McAnearney, Wright
Bailey drops Brian Carter's cross and George Kirby nets after a scramble. Leadbetter centres and Crawford launches into a handsome diving header to level. Geoff Barnsley parries a shot and Crawford tucks in his 20th goal in 21 matches. The otherwise quiet Phillips nets a late third.

LEAGUE DIVISION 2

Manager: Alf Ramsey

SEASON 1960-61

No	Date		Att	Pos	Pt	F-A	H-T	Scorers, Times, and Referees	1	2	3	4	5	6	7	8	9	10	11
22	17/12	H LEYTON ORIENT W 3	9,803	20	29	6-2	2-0	Craw '6,62,80, Owen 27'(og), Lead' 75, Johnston 53, McD' 73 [Phillips 89p] Ref: K Stokes	Bailey *George*	Carberry *Eagles*	Malcolm *Charlton*	Pickett *Gibson*	Nelson *Owen*	Elsworthy *Lea*	Stephenson *Waites*	Millward *Gibbs*	Crawford *Johnston*	Phillips *Johnston*	Leadbetter *Elwood*
23	26/12	A NORWICH W 2	30,884	6	31	3-0	2-0	Crawford 22, 70, Phillips 37, Ref: M Fussey	Bailey *Kennon*	Carberry *Thurlow*	Malcolm *Ashman*	Pickett *McCrohan*	Nelson *Butler*	Elsworthy *Crowe*	Stephenson *Crossan*	Millward *Lythgoe*	Crawford *Allcock*	Phillips *Hill*	Leadbetter *Punton*
24	27/12	H NORWICH W 1	23,321	7	33	4-1	2-1	Phillips 27p, Crawford 39, 72, Hill 18 [Millward 85] Ref: A Mason	Bailey *Kennon*	Carberry *Thurlow*	Baxter *Ashman*	Pickett *McCrohan*	Nelson *Butler*	Elsworthy *Crowe*	Stephenson *Whitehouse*	Millward *Larkin*	Crawford *Allcock*	Phillips *Hill*	Leadbetter *Punton*
25	14/1	H BRISTOL ROV W 2	11,946	20	35	3-2	2-1	Millward 11, Stephenson 32, 53, Biggs 13, 49, Ref: R Leafe	Bailey *Radford*	Carberry *Hillard*	Malcolm *Frowen*	Pickett *Sampson*	Nelson *Pyle*	Baxter *Mabbutt*	Stephenson *Jarman*	Millward *Biggs*	Crawford *Sykes*	Phillips *Hooper*	Leadbetter *Petherbridge*
26	21/1	A LIVERPOOL D 2	33,401	3	36	1-1	1-0	Phillips 42, Lewis 73, Ref: J Powell	Bailey *Slater*	Carberry *Molyneux*	Malcolm *Byrne*	Pickett *Milne*	Nelson *White*	Elsworthy *Leishman*	Stephenson *Lewis*	Millward *Hunt*	Crawford *Hickson*	Phillips *Harrower*	Leadbetter *A'Court*
27	4/2	H ROTHERHAM D 2	12,225	15	37	1-1	1-1	Crawford 21, Sawyer 9, Ref: F Reid	Bailey *Wren*	Carberry *Perry*	Malcolm *Morgan*	Baxter *Lambert*	Nelson *Madden*	Elsworthy *Waterhouse*	Stephenson *Webster*	Millward *Kirkman*	Crawford *Sawyer*	Phillips *Weston*	Leadbetter *Bambridge*
28	11/2	A SOUTHAMPTON D 2	19,946	4	38	1-1	0-1	Stephenson 64, O'Brien 43p, Ref: D Smith	Bailey *Reynolds*	Carberry *Davies*	Malcolm *Traynor*	Baxter *Connor*	Nelson *Page*	Elsworthy *Huxford*	Stephenson *Paine*	Millward *O'Brien*	Crawford *Reeves*	Phillips *Mulgrew*	Leadbetter *Penk*
29	18/2	H LEEDS W 2	13,125	10	40	4-0	3-0	Crawford 16, Phillips 36, 43, Rees 54 Ref: H New	Bailey *Humphries*	Carberry *Jones*	Malcolm *Hair*	Baxter *Cameron*	Nelson *Charlton*	Elsworthy *Goodwin*	Stephenson *Francis*	Millward *Smith*	Crawford *McCole*	Phillips *Bremner*	Leadbetter *Hawksby*
30	25/2	H CHARLTON W 2	14,365	13	42	2-1	1-1	Crawford 23, 63, Summers 26 Ref: T Dawes	Bailey *Duff*	Carberry *Sewell*	Malcolm *Townsend*	Baxter *Hewie*	Nelson *Jago*	Elsworthy *Tocknell*	Stephenson *Lawrie*	Millward *Edwards*	Crawford *Leary*	Phillips *White*	Leadbetter *Summers*
31	7/3	A SHEFFIELD UTD W 1	35,057	2	44	3-1	1-0	Phillips 32, Crawford 51, 66, Simpson 56 Ref: T Reynolds	Bailey *Hodgkinson*	Carberry *Caldwell*	Malcolm *Shaw G*	Baxter *Richardson*	Nelson *Shaw J*	Elsworthy *Summers*	Stephenson *Hodgson*	Millward *Russell*	Crawford *Pace*	Phillips *Kettleborough*	Leadbetter *Simpson*

22 Crawford fires home after a corner, before a Phillips shot is diverted into his own net by Trefor Owen. Tom Johnston backheels a neat goal but Crawford's brilliant shot restores the cushion. Terry McDonald makes the most of a mix-up to net, but Town finish with an emphatic flourish.

23 City gain 15 corners to Town's one, but Archie Macauley's men lose their one-year unbeaten run at home thanks to lethal finishing. Crawford turns and shoots the opener. Phillips nips in to punish a poor Ron Ashman back-pass. Crawford scores after a Phillips thunderbolt is blocked.

24 Terry Allcock's lob sends Jim Hill through to score. Barry Butler handles and Phillips thrashes in his 12th penalty from 12 attempts. Crawford snaps a typical brace in his 100th first-team match. Millward hammers home a well-created goal to ensure Town go back to the top of the table.

25 Millward stretches to score but Alfie Biggs levels with a header. Stephenson nets after Millward's shot is blocked, but Biggs cracks in another. Stephenson's header regains the lead. A bizarre miss is put down to 'putter's twitch' as Biggs unaccountably hesitates in front of an open goal.

26 Town match Bill Shankly's team in a real thriller. The energetic Crawford sets up a handsome Phillips strike to shock the partisan home crowd. Dave Hickson sets up Kevin Lewis, who gives Bailey no chance. Gallant Town deserve a point and Nelson and Bailey are outstanding.

27 Brian Sawyer nods in a floated Barry Webster cross. Crawford glides in a centre from Leadbetter, who is playing his 112th consecutive first team game, and has only missed three in the last 212. A point goes begging when Jack Wren saves a Phillips penalty – his first miss in 13 tries.

28 George O'Brien fires a spot-kick in off the bar after Mr Smith rules that he was impeded by Elsworthy, a verdict Ramsey firmly disagrees with. Crawford and Phillips miss several chances, but Stephenson nets a firm drive to give a measure of revenge for the FA Cup hammering.

29 Glorious headers by Crawford and Phillips demoralise the visitors. It gets even better when the pair carve Leeds apart with a series of headers back and forth before Phillips volleys in a sensational goal. Leeds look on in sheer disbelief. Rees marks his return with a comfortable fourth.

30 Phillips and Rees miss good chances and Bailey has to work hard to keep Town in the game. Crawford shows sharp reactions to pounce and score after Billy Duff parries Stephenson's effort. John Summers equalises after a Carberry howler. Crawford wins both points with a header.

31 Amid high tension, Crawford feeds Phillips whose finish is lethal. Crawford forces a second as he collides with Brian Richardson. A fine solo effort by Ron Simpson is forgotten as Crawford nets from close in. The best-ever display by an Ipswich team, crows joyful chairman Cobbold.

Ipswich Town — Season Results (continued)

No	H/A	Date	Opponent		Res	Score		Pos	Pts	Att
32	H	11/3	STOKE		W	2-1	1-0	1 17	46	16,578
33	A	18/3	PLYMOUTH (at Torquay)		W	2-1	1-1	1 8	48	9,879
34	H	25/3	LUTON		L	0-1	0-1	1 12	48	21,744
35	H	31/3	MIDDLESBROUGH		W	3-1	2-1	1 5	50	22,239
36	A	1/4	HUDDERSFIELD		W	3-1	1-0	1 20	52	16,459
37	A	3/4	MIDDLESBROUGH		L	1-3	0-1	1 5	52	12,996
38	H	8/4	PORTSMOUTH		D	2-2	2-2	1 21	53	18,538
39	A	15/4	LINCOLN		W	4-1	0-1	1 22	55	7,820
40	H	22/4	SUNDERLAND		W	4-0	2-0	1 6	57	21,115
41	A	24/4	DERBY		W	4-1	0-1	1 12	59	13,121
42	A	29/4	SWANSEA		L	1-2	0-1	1 7	59	18,239

Average: Home 15,095, Away 16,148

Match details

32. STOKE — Phillips 12, Elsworthy 90; *King 66* — Ref: J Williams
Town: Bailey, Carberry, Malcolm, Baxter, Nelson, Elsworthy, Stephenson, Rees, Crawford, Phillips, Leadbetter
Stoke: *O'Neill, Asprey, Allen, Howitt, Andrews, Skeels, Anderson, Mudie, Bullock, Ratcliffe, King*
Peter Bullock fluffs a sitter and moments later Phillips shows him how it's done. John King fires a neat equaliser for Tony Waddington's men. In injury-time Town win a hotly-disputed corner; in the ensuing panic the ball falls to Elsworthy, whose gentle lob forward floats into the net.

33. PLYMOUTH (at Torquay) — Phillips 20, Crawford 85; *Carter 22* — Ref: R Smith
Town: Bailey, Carberry, Malcolm, Baxter, Nelson, Elsworthy, Stephenson, Rees, Crawford, Phillips, Leadbetter
Plymouth: *Barnsley, Wyatt, Fulton, Williams, Fincham, Newman, Carter, Anderson, Kirby, McAnearney, Malloy*
The FA has closed Home Park for 14 days due to crowd misdemeanours. Ramsey agrees to Plymouth's late request to play at Torquay, even though plans had been made to use White Hart Lane. A poor game is settled near time when Crawford pounces on an error by Geoff Barnsley.

34. LUTON — ; *McGuffie 20* — Ref: M Jordan
Town: Bailey, Carberry, Malcolm, Baxter, Nelson, Elsworthy, Stephenson, Rees, Crawford, Phillips, Leadbetter
Luton: *Baynham, McNally, Bramwell, Morton, Kelly, Groves, McCann, McGuffie, Turner, Cummins, Fleming*
To avoid a clash with the Grand National, this kicks-off at 7pm. Nelson heads a clearance straight to Alwyn McGuffie who accepts the gift. Keeper Ron Baynham - recently recovered from a fractured skull - makes several fine saves and Town tumble to their first defeat in 16 weeks.

35. MIDDLESBROUGH — Leadbetter 5, Crawford 16, 83; *Peacock 23* — Ref: J Cooke
Town: Bailey, Carberry, Malcolm, Baxter, Nelson, Elsworthy, Stephenson, Rees, Crawford, Phillips, Leadbetter
Middlesbrough: *Million, Jones, McNeil, Yeoman, Thomson, Horner, Kaye, Hamilton, Clough, Peacock, Holliday*
After a minute's silence for the late FA Council chairman Arthur Drewery, Town tear into Bob Dennison's men. Leadbetter chests in the first and then Crawford nets a diving header. Alan Peacock reduces the arrears from a free-kick. Near the end Crawford glides in a clinching goal.

36. HUDDERSFIELD — Phillips 17, 59, Crawford 70; *McHale 88* — Ref: W Surtees
Town: Bailey, Carberry, Malcolm, Baxter, Nelson, Elsworthy, Stephenson, Rees, Crawford, Phillips, Leadbetter
Huddersfield: *Fearnley, Parker, Wilson, Saward, Coddington, Dinsdale, McHale, Balderstone, Kerray, Massie, O'Grady*
A cracking opening goal sees Phillips drive past Harry Fearnley after good work by Crawford. Big Ted produces another thunderbolt for the second and Crawford makes sure of the win, following in a Rees effort. A fine display is only slightly marred by Kevin McHale's consolation.

37. MIDDLESBROUGH — Phillips 60; *Yeoman 25, Holliday 88p, Clough 90* — Ref: L Tirebuck
Town: Bailey, Carberry, Malcolm, Baxter, Nelson, Elsworthy, Stephenson, Rees, Crawford, Phillips, Leadbetter
Middlesbrough: *Million, Jones, McNeil, Yeoman, Thomson, Horner, Kaye, Hamilton, Clough, Peacock, Holliday*
Brian Clough's close-range drive hits Bailey in the face and knocks him out. The dazed keeper is beaten moments later by a Ramon Yeoman 25-yarder. Town draw level via a Phillips gem, made by Crawford. Boro strike late, with Clough making the most of a real defensive howler.

38. PORTSMOUTH — Phillips 2p, Curtis 25; *Cutler 1, Howells 27* — Ref: K Stokes
Town: Bailey, Carberry, Malcolm, Baxter, Nelson, Elsworthy, Stephenson, Curtis, Crawford, Phillips, Leadbetter
Portsmouth: *Beattie, Rutter, Wilson, Howells, Snadon, Dickinson, Campbell, Gordon, Saunders, Brown, Cutler*
Promotion is now tantalisingly close but Town fall behind within a minute as Reg Cutler forces in a corner. Moments later Cyril Rutter shoves Phillips and Town are level. Curtis's header is quickly followed by a firm Ron Howells shot. The goals are shown on BBC's Sports Special.

39. LINCOLN — Crawf'd 78, Phillips 50, Leadbetter 52, [Stephenson 86]; Punter 17 [Curtis 87] — Ref: J Bullough
Town: Bailey, Carberry, Malcolm, Baxter, Nelson, Elsworthy, Stephenson, Curtis, Crawford, Phillips, Leadbetter
Lincoln: *Heath, Barnard, Smith, Middleton, Jackson, Drysdale, McClelland, Holmes, Punter, Chapman, Bannister*
A big Town following is shocked as Brian Punter forces in an opener for the lowly Imps. Phillips nets after Bill Heath drops a cross, and after furious protests the ref changes his original decision and allows the goal. Town cruise home from here and promotion is virtually a certainty.

40. SUNDERLAND — Elsworthy 4, Crawford 38, Curtis 48, [Phillips 80p] — Ref: M Fussey
Town: Bailey, Carberry, Malcolm, Baxter, Nelson, Elsworthy, Stephenson, Curtis, Crawford, Phillips, Leadbetter
Sunderland: *Wakeham, Nelson, Ashurst, Anderson, Rooks, McNab, Davison, Fogarty, Lawther, McPheat, Dillon*
The party commences when Pete Wakeham allows Elsworthy's header to drift over him. Unmarked Crawford heads a second. Curtis steams in to head another and a perfect day is complete after Dickie Rooks' handball. Alf Ramsey's appeal for no pitch invasions is joyfully ignored.

41. DERBY — Stephenson 69, 81, Crawford 86, Hutchinson 6 [Curtis 87] — Ref: J Cattlin
Town: Bailey, Carberry, Malcolm, Baxter, Nelson, Elsworthy, Stephenson, Curtis, Crawford, Phillips, Leadbetter
Derby: *Oxford, Barrowcliffe, Conwell, Parry, Young, Upton, Swallow, Thompson, Curry, Hutchinson, Fagan*
Promotion's in the bag, now for the title! Barry Hutchinson nets a neat backheel, but the championship is clinched thanks to a storming last 21 minutes. Stephenson's powerful drive is followed by three classic poachers' goals. Loud singing is reported from the visitors' dressing room!

42. SWANSEA — Phillips 50; *Nurse 7, Reynolds 88* — Ref: K Dagnall
Town: Bailey, Carberry, Malcolm, Baxter, Nelson, Elsworthy, Stephenson, Curtis, Crawford, Phillips, Leadbetter
Swansea: *King, Sanders, Griffiths, Johnson, Nurse, Davies P, Jones, Morgan, Reynolds, Webster, Williams*
Trevor Morris's side form a guard of honour to welcome the champions onto the pitch. Mel Nurse is less hospitable, hammering in a free-kick. Phillips nets Town's 100th goal of the season with a glorious 20-yarder, but an excellent game is won by Brayley Reynolds' opportunist effort.

LEAGUE DIVISION 2 (CUP-TIES) Manager: Alf Ramsey SEASON 1960-61

League Cup

			F-A	H-T	Scorers, Times, and Referees	1	2	3	4	5	6	7	8	9	10	11
1	H	BARNSLEY	2 L 0-2	0-2		Bailey	Carberry	Malcolm	Pickett	Laurel	Elsworthy	Siddall	Millward	Crawford	Phillips	Leadbetter
		11,189 3:8			Beaumont 5, Bartlett 39	Leeson	Swift	Brookes E	Barber	Sharpe	Houghton	Smillie	Bartlett	Stainsby	Beaumont	Brookes C
					Ref: C Woan											

A new competition is launched and Town are humbled by Johnny Steele's lowly Third Division side. Frank Beaumont nets an early header from a corner, the first opposition goal under the new floodlights. Off-colour Elsworthy dithers to allow Frank Bartlett in to score the second.

FA Cup

			F-A	H-T	Scorers, Times, and Referees	1	2	3	4	5	6	7	8	9	10	11
3	A	SOUTHAMPTON	2 L 1-7	0-6	Page 47 (og) [Penk 30, Paine 39]	Bailey	Carberry	Malcolm	Pickett	Nelson	Elsworthy	Stephenson	Millward	Crawford	Phillips	Leadbetter
		20,422 7			O'Brien 7, 26p, 29, Mulgrew 22, 78.	Reynolds	Davies	Traynor	Connor	Page	Huxford	Paine	O'Brien	Reeves	Mulgrew	Penk
					Ref: C Rogers											

Nelson's blunder allows George O'Brien to cash in. Town are then destroyed by five goals in just 13 minutes. O'Brien snaps up a hat-trick and Terry Paine hammers in a fierce drive. The only consolation is when Stephenson's shot is deflected in. It's a club record defeat in the FA Cup.

League Table

	Team	P	Home					Away					Pts
			W	D	L	F	A	W	D	L	F	A	
1	IPSWICH	42	15	3	3	55	24	11	4	6	45	31	59
2	Sheffield Utd	42	16	2	3	49	22	10	4	7	32	29	58
3	Liverpool	42	14	5	2	49	21	7	5	9	38	37	52
4	Norwich	42	15	3	3	46	20	5	6	10	24	33	49
5	Middlesbro	42	13	6	2	44	20	5	6	10	39	54	48
6	Sunderland	42	12	5	4	47	24	5	8	8	28	36	47
7	Swansea	42	14	4	3	49	26	4	7	10	28	47	47
8	Southampton	42	12	4	5	57	35	6	4	11	27	46	44
9	Scunthorpe	42	9	8	4	39	25	5	7	9	30	39	43
10	Charlton	42	12	3	6	60	42	4	8	9	37	49	43
11	Plymouth	42	13	4	4	52	32	4	4	13	29	50	42
12	Derby	42	9	6	6	46	35	6	4	11	34	45	40
13	Luton	42	13	5	3	48	27	3	2	16	23	52	39
14	Leeds	42	9	7	5	41	38	3	7	11	28	40	38
15	Rotherham	42	9	7	5	37	24	3	6	12	28	49	37
16	Brighton	42	9	6	6	33	26	5	3	13	28	49	37
17	Bristol Rov	42	13	4	4	52	35	2	3	16	21	57	37
18	Stoke	42	9	6	6	39	26	3	6	12	12	33	36
19	Leyton O	42	10	5	6	31	29	4	3	14	24	49	36
20	Huddersfield	42	7	5	9	33	33	6	4	11	29	38	35
21	Portsmouth	42	10	6	5	38	27	1	5	15	26	64	33
22	Lincoln	42	5	4	12	30	43	3	4	14	18	52	24
		924	246	108	108	975	634	108	108	246	634	975	924

Odds & ends

Double wins: (10) L Orient, Derby, Brighton, Leeds, Stoke, Charlton, Lincoln, Huddersfield, Plymouth, Norwich.

Double losses: (2) Luton and Swansea.

Won from behind: (8) Derby (h), Leeds (a), Stoke (a), Huddersfield (h), Plymouth (h), Norwich (h), Lincoln (a), Derby (a).

Lost from in front: (0).

High spots: Beating the big city clubs to the title.
The lethal Crawford-Phillips partnership yielding 70 goals.
A glorious seven-goal Christmas against local enemies Norwich!
The crucial victory at title rivals Sheffield United in March.
The sensational third goal in the home win over Leeds.

Low spots: Losing 1-7 at Southampton - a club record FA Cup defeat.
The inept display at Scunthorpe in August.
Winger Peter Berry being forced to quit at 27 due to injury.

Hat-tricks: (3) Ray Crawford v Brighton, Leeds and Leyton Orient.
Opposing hat-tricks: (1) George O'Brien v Southampton (FAC).
Ever-presents: (4) Carberry, Crawford, Leadbetter, Phillips.
Leading scorer: Ray Crawford (40).

Appearances and Goals

Player	Appearances			Goals			
	Lge	LC	FAC	Lge	LC	FAC	Tot
Bailey, Roy	38	1	1				
Baxter, Billy	19						
Carberry, Larry	42		1				
Crawford, Ray	42	1	1	40			40
Compton, John	3						
Curtis, Dermot	5			3			3
Elsworthy, John	39	1	1	3			3
Hall, Wilf	4						
Laurel, John	3						
Leadbetter, Jimmy	42	1	1	3			3
Malcolm, Ken	41		1				
Millward, Doug	19	1	1	6			6
Nelson, Andy	39		1				
Owen, Aled	8			1			1
Phillips, Ted	42	1	1	30			30
Pickett, Reg	24	1	1				
Rees, Derek	16			4			4
Siddall, Brian	3						
Stephenson, Roy	33		1	9			9
(own-goals)				1		1	2
19 players used	462	11	11	100		1	101

LEAGUE DIVISION 1 — Manager: Alf Ramsey — SEASON 1961-62

Match details

No	Venue/Opponent	Date	Att	Pos	Pt	F-A	H-T	Scorers, Times, and Referees
1	A BOLTON	19/8	16,708		D 1	0-0	0-0	Ref: F Allott
2	A BURNLEY	22/8	24,577		L 1	3-4	1-2	Phillips 38, 73, Craw' 52 /McIlroy 77/ Pointer 23, Harris 42, Miller 64, Ref: R Langdale
3	H MANCHESTER C	26/8	21,473	19 / 2	L 1	2-4	2-2	Betts 34 (og), Leadbetter 44 /Barlow 13, Hayes 36, Dobing 86, 87/ Ref: M Fussey
4	H BURNLEY	29/8	23,835	11 / 7	W 3	6-2	3-1	Cr' 3, 65, St' 12, Mo' 22, Ph' 49, L'73 /McIlroy 11, Elsworthy 87 (og)/ Ref: K Stokes
5	A WEST BROM	2/9	19,016	9 / 22	W 5	3-1	2-0	Moran 21, 89, Crawford 42 /Jackson 62/ Ref: G McCabe
6	H BLACKBURN	5/9	24,928	6 / 14	W 7	2-1	2-1	Stephenson 13, Phillips 22 /Douglas 41p/ Ref: K Aston
7	H BIRMINGHAM	9/9	20,017	5 / 21	W 9	4-1	2-1	Crawford 2, Phillips 19, 54, Moran 84 /Singer 12/ Ref: A Mason
8	A EVERTON	16/9	35,259	7 / 18	L 9	2-5	0-2	Phillips 72, Moran 77 /Bingham 69/ Temple 18, 30, 84, Young 48, Ref: P Brandwood
9	A BLACKBURN	18/9	19,904	5 / 8	D 10	2-2	1-1	Phillips 13p, 79 /Lawther 40, McEvoy 73/ Ref: R Windle
10	H FULHAM	23/9	23,050	8 / 6	L 10	2-4	1-1	Crawford 22, 70 /O'Connell 72/ Cook 38, Cohen 52, Haynes 55, Ref: J Cook

Line-ups (1–11; opponents in italics)

No	1	2	3	4	5	6	7	8	9	10	11
1	Bailey	Carberry	Malcolm	Baxter	Nelson	Elsworthy	Stephenson	Moran	Crawford	Phillips	Leadbetter
	Hopkinson	*Hartle*	*Farrimond*	*Rimmer*	*Edwards*	*Wilkinson*	*Holden*	*Stevens*	*McAdams*	*Hill*	*Pilkington*
2	Bailey	Carberry	Malcolm	Baxter	Nelson	Elsworthy	Stephenson	Moran	Crawford	Phillips	Leadbetter
	Blacklaw	*Angus*	*Elder*	*Adamson*	*Cummings*	*Miller*	*Connelly*	*McIlroy*	*Pointer*	*Robson*	*Harris*
3	Bailey	Carberry	Malcolm	Baxter	Nelson	Elsworthy	Stephenson	Moran	Crawford	Phillips	Leadbetter
	Trautmann	*Betts*	*Leivers*	*Cheetham*	*Ewing*	*Kennedy*	*Barlow*	*Dobing*	*Baker*	*Hayes*	*Wagstaffe*
4	Bailey	Carberry	Compton	Baxter	Nelson	Elsworthy	Stephenson	Moran	Crawford	Phillips	Leadbetter
	Blacklaw	*Angus*	*Elder*	*Adamson*	*Cummings*	*Miller*	*Connelly*	*McIlroy*	*Pointer*	*Robson*	*Towers*
5	Bailey	Carberry	Compton	Baxter	Nelson	Elsworthy	Stephenson	Moran	Crawford	Phillips	Leadbetter
	Wallace	*Howe*	*Williams*	*Robson*	*Jones*	*Drury*	*Jackson*	*Hope*	*Smith*	*Kevan*	*Clarke*
6	Bailey	Carberry	Compton	Baxter	Nelson	Elsworthy	Stephenson	Moran	Crawford	Phillips	Leadbetter
	Else	*Bray*	*Newton*	*Clayton*	*Woods*	*McGrath*	*Isherwood*	*Crowe*	*Pickering*	*Douglas*	*Haverty*
7	Bailey	Withers	Compton	Baxter	Nelson	Elsworthy	Stephenson	Moran	Crawford	Phillips	Leadbetter
		Foster	*Allen*	*Watts*	*Smith*	*Beard*	*Hellawell*	*Bloomfield*	*Harris*	*Singer*	*Taylor*
8	Hall	Carberry	Compton	Baxter	Nelson	Elsworthy	Stephenson	Moran	Crawford	Phillips	Leadbetter
	Dunlop	*Parker*	*Thomson*	*Gabriel*	*Labone*	*Harris*	*Bingham*	*Young*	*Wignall*	*Temple*	*Fell*
9	Hall	Carberry	Compton	Baxter	Nelson	Elsworthy	Stephenson	Moran	Crawford	Phillips	Leadbetter
	Reeves	*Bray*	*Newton*	*Clayton*	*Woods*	*McEvoy*	*Isherwood*	*Crowe*	*Lawther*	*Douglas*	*Haverty*
10	Hall	Carberry	Compton	Baxter	Nelson	Elsworthy	Stephenson	Moran	Crawford	Phillips	Leadbetter
	Macedo	*Cohen*	*Langley*	*Mullery*	*Dodgin*	*Lowe*	*Key*	*O'Connell*	*Cook*	*Haynes*	*Chamberlain*

Match reports

1. Town's first top-flight game and Moran from Falkirk debuts. Bill Ridding's Burnden Park side struggle to compete with a fine half-back display by Baxter, Nelson and Elsworthy. Bailey's handling is top class. He is beaten by Dennis Stevens, but the effort is disallowed for a foul.

2. A magnificent contest sparks into life as Ray Pointer nets from close range. Three times Town cancel out a Clarets lead. Jim McIlroy swoops on a defensive error to win the points. Ramsey brushes aside his disappointment to call it 'wonderful' and the best Town display he's witnessed.

3. The Coldstream Guards band is a prelude to another thriller that Town are unlucky to lose. Colin Barlow is set up by Peter Dobing, but a Barrie Betts back-pass drifts over Bert Trautmann to level it. A Town pass hits the ref and falls for Dobing to hit the first of two decisive late strikes.

4. Stand-in Compton is a revelation in his first game at full-back as Town turn on the style. Jimmy McIlroy's flick cancels out Crawford's early drive, but Stephenson responds instantly with a shot that deflects in off Brian Miller. Moran heads a third and rampant Town never look back.

5. Crawford heads Baxter's cross over a stranded Jock Wallace for Moran to nod in a simple opener. Crawford nutmegs Graham Williams and lashes home a fierce shot. Alec Jackson appears to handle but is allowed to go on and beat Bailey. Moran volleys home a late clinching goal.

6. Phillips and Moran both have efforts blocked but Stephenson is on hand to convert. Town go two ahead when a superb move sees Leadbetter lay the ball back for Phillips to crash in a terrific piledriver. Baxter's challenge on Bryan Douglas is deemed a penalty, much to Town's fury.

7. Carberry's pass carves City open for Crawford to expertly convert. Jimmy Bloomfield engineers a James Singer equaliser for Gil Merrick's lads. A Phillips thunderbolt restores the lead and after the break he is put clear for his second. Moran nets from close range after a corner kick.

8. Town are overrun, apart from a brief late comeback bid. Derek Temple collects a fine hat-trick, his first a cracking solo effort. The Golden Vision, a.k.a. Alex Young, kills off any lingering hopes. Moran sets up Phillips and then nets a header himself, but Temple has the last laugh.

9. Matt Woods handles for Phillips' penalty. Ian Lawther fires in from 18 yards to level. Stand-in Andy McEvoy wallops in a tremendous volley from distance. Jack Marshall's side are pegged back when Compton's chip is punched out by Brian Reeves, but rebounds in off Phillips' face!

10. Maestro Johnny Haynes gives a great display after Fulham recover from Crawford's headed opener. George Cohen lashes in a rare goal before Haynes himself nets after a neat passing movement. Tony Macedo slips up for Town's second, but Pat O'Connell's header ends Town hopes.

No		Opponent	Date			Res		Score	HT	Scorers / Ref
11	A	SHEFFIELD WED	30/9	26,565	6 / 9	W	12	4-1	3-1	Phillips 4, 63, Crawford 15, Lead '35 / Fantham 25 — Ref: E Norman
12	H	WEST HAM	7/10	28,059	4 / 3	W	14	4-2	0-0	Crawford 57, 66, Phillips 64, 73 / Sealey 70, Musgrove 88 — Ref: P Brandwood
13	A	SHEFFIELD UTD	14/10	22,194	6 / 13	L	14	1-2	1-2	Leadbetter 30 / Russell 12, Pace 42 — Ref: L Hamer
14	H	TOTTENHAM	21/10	28,778	4 / 6	W	16	3-2	1-2	Phillips 37, Crawford 54, 56 / Jones 21, 44 — Ref: R Tinkler
15	A	BLACKPOOL	28/10	19,773	4 / 14	D	17	1-1	1-0	Phillips 32 / Parry 83 — Ref: A Luty
16	H	NOTT'M FOREST	4/11	19,068	3 / 13	W	19	1-0	1-0	Phillips 23 — Ref: G Pullin
17	A	WOLVERHAMPTON	11/11	21,711	5 / 15	L	19	0-2	0-0	Wharton 69, Hinton 82 — Ref: P Bye
18	H	MANCHESTER U	18/11	25,755	3 / 18	W	21	4-1	1-0	Phillips 26, 67, Crawford 73 / McMillan 90 [Elsworthy 86] — Ref: K Aston
19	A	CARDIFF	25/11	22,823	2 / 12	W	23	3-0	2-0	Phillips 8, 84, Moran 42 — Ref: J Kelly
20	H	CHELSEA	2/12	22,762	2 / 22	W	25	5-2	2-1	Crawford 4, 52, 74, Moran 15 / Tambling 6, Murray 66 [Steph'son 78] — Ref: P Bye
21	A	ASTON VILLA	9/12	31,924	3 / 7	L	25	0-3	0-1	McParland 26, 47, Thomson 82 — Ref: F Cowan

Line-ups (home line listed first, opponents in italics)

	Hall/Bailey	Carberry	Compton	Baxter	Nelson	Elsworthy	Stephenson	Moran	Crawford	Phillips	Leadbetter
11	Hall	Carberry	Compton	Baxter	Nelson	Elsworthy	Stephenson	Moran	Crawford	Phillips	Leadbetter
	Springett	*Johnson*	*Megson*	*McAnearney*	*Swann*	*Kay*	*Wilkinson*	*Craig*	*Ellis*	*Fantham*	*Dobson*
12	Bailey	Carberry	Compton	Baxter	Nelson	Elsworthy	Stephenson	Moran	Crawford	Phillips	Leadbetter
	Leslie	*Kirkup*	*Bond*	*Hurst*	*Brown*	*Moore*	*Scott*	*Woosnam*	*Sealey*	*Dick*	*Musgrove*
13	Bailey	Carberry	Compton	Baxter	Nelson	Elsworthy	Stephenson	Moran	Crawford	Phillips	Leadbetter
	Hopkinson	*Coldwell*	*Shaw G*	*Richardson*	*Shaw J*	*Summers*	*Allchurch*	*Russell*	*Pace*	*Simpson*	*Hartle*
14	Bailey	Carberry	Compton	Baxter	Nelson	Elsworthy	Stephenson	Moran	Crawford	Phillips	Leadbetter
	Brown	*Baker*	*Henry*	*Blanchflower*	*Norman*	*Mackay*	*Jones*	*White*	*Smith*	*Allen*	*Dyson*
15	Bailey	Carberry	Compton	Baxter	Nelson	Elsworthy	Stephenson	Moran	Crawford	Phillips	Leadbetter
	Waiters	*Armfield*	*Martin*	*Crawford*	*Gratrix*	*Durie*	*Hill*	*Peterson*	*Charnley*	*Parry*	*Horne*
16	Bailey	Carberry	Compton	Baxter	Nelson	Elsworthy	Stephenson	Moran	Crawford	Phillips	Leadbetter
	Grummitt	*Baird*	*Palmer*	*Grant*	*McKinlay*	*Whitefoot*	*Vowden*	*Booth*	*Addison*	*Quigley*	*Le Flem*
17	Bailey	Carberry	Compton	Baxter	Nelson	Elsworthy	Stephenson	Moran	Crawford	Phillips	Leadbetter
	Finlayson	*Stewart*	*Harris*	*Clamp*	*Slater*	*Flowers*	*Wharton*	*Mason*	*Murray*	*Broadbent*	*Hinton*
18	Bailey	Carberry	Compton	Baxter	Nelson	Elsworthy	Curtis	Moran	Crawford	Phillips	Leadbetter
	Gaskell	*Brennan*	*Dunne*	*Stiles*	*Foulkes*	*Setters*	*Bradley*	*Giles*	*Herd*	*Charlton*	*McMillan*
19	Bailey	Carberry	Compton	Baxter	Nelson	Elsworthy	Stephenson	Moran	Crawford	Phillips	Leadbetter
	John	*Harrington*	*Milne*	*Hole*	*Rankmore*	*Baker*	*King P*	*Tapscott*	*King J*	*Ward*	*Hogg*
20	Bailey	Carberry	Compton	Baxter	Nelson	Elsworthy	Stephenson	Moran	Crawford	Phillips	Leadbetter
	Bonetti	*Shellito*	*Harris*	*Malcolm*	*Scott*	*Bradley*	*Murray*	*Tambling*	*Brabrook*	*Bridges*	*Blunstone*
21	Bailey	Carberry	Compton	Baxter	Nelson	Elsworthy	Stephenson	Moran	Crawford	Phillips	Leadbetter
	Sims	*Lee*	*Aitken*	*Crowe*	*Sleeuwenhoek*	*Deakin*	*McParland*	*Wylie*	*Thomson*	*Dougan*	*O'Neill*

11 — A SHEFFIELD WED (30/9): Phillips marks 200 games by holding off defenders to net a Carberry pass. Crawford fires in a Leadbetter lay-back before Johnny Fantham scrambles one back. Leadbetter nets a well-placed shot. Phillips gets clear and nets what he later calls probably his most powerful shot to date!

12 — H WEST HAM (7/10): Goals aplenty again as a purple patch of 16 minutes yields four Town goals. Crawford's pair includes a rebound after a Phillips 25-yarder is too hot for Lawrie Leslie. Alan Sealey's long-range rocket is academic. Winger Stephenson has a hand in most attacks and torments John Bond.

13 — A SHEFFIELD UTD (14/10): Defensive hesitation lets in Billy Russell to put Johnny Harris's men ahead. After a Crawford effort is blocked, Leadbetter strides forward to drive in a firm shot. Bailey gets down to parry a Blades free-kick, but the ball falls to the feet of the lethal 'Doc' Pace who makes no mistake.

14 — H TOTTENHAM (21/10): The reigning champions pull in a record gate and a classic ensues. Cliff Jones' diving header is cancelled out a by a mighty Phillips left-footer, but the Welshman heads another. Crawford swoops twice with delightful finishes and shrugs his shoulders at the fans as if to say 'no problem!'

15 — A BLACKPOOL (28/10): Jimmy Armfield goes off with a leg injury, returning later to limp around at centre-forward. A Leadbetter cross is headed in by Phillips and things look good for Town. Seven minutes from time, the victory is snatched away when Ray Parry crashes home a Ray Charnley knock-down.

16 — H NOTT'M FOREST (4/11): Town are relieved when John Quigley's diving header is disallowed for offside. Leadbetter lobs into the danger area and after Crawford and Baird miss the ball, Phillips arrives to steer it in. After 75 minutes Geoff Vowden is hauled down, but Calvin Palmer's penalty is palmed away.

17 — A WOLVERHAMPTON (11/11): In the opening minutes Town suffer a serious blow as Stephenson goes off with a strained thigh. The remaining ten men put on an admirable rearguard action, but are sunk in the final quarter. Stan Cullis put faith in two teenage wingers and both net emphatic efforts past brave Bailey.

18 — H MANCHESTER U (18/11): England boss Walter Winterbottom comes to see the shooting prowess of Phillips, who is fast becoming the talk of the nation. Ted nets two typical scorchers and Town are toying with Matt Busby's men by the end. Elsworthy's free-kick spins freakishly past a horrified Dave Gaskell.

19 — A CARDIFF (25/11): A truly extraordinary opening goal as Phillips shoots from massive distance and a tight angle and sees it dip and swerve into the net. He's now the League's leading scorer. Moran's shot goes in via Frank Rankmore. Phillips' downward header seals a miserable day for Bill Jones's outfit.

20 — H CHELSEA (2/12): Ted Drake's lowly side look impressive for long periods, but Town's finishing is lethal. Crawford makes up for his disappointing England debut by firing through a forest of legs to complete the first Town hat-trick this term. Stephenson rifles home the team's 52nd goal in 20 games.

21 — A ASTON VILLA (9/12): Town are unable to deal adequately with the in-form Peter McParland and Joe Mercer's team rarely look in trouble. The crucial second goal is the result of a defensive howler. Skipper Nelson is given a torrid time by the unconventional Derek Dougan, a recent capture from Blackburn.

LEAGUE DIVISION 1 — Manager: Alf Ramsey — SEASON 1961-62

22. H BOLTON 16/12 — Att 16,587 — Pos 2 — Pt 27 (W) — F-A 2-1 — H-T 0-1
Town: Bailey, Carberry, Compton, Baxter, Nelson, Elsworthy, Stephenson, Moran, Crawford, Phillips, Leadbetter
Bolton: Hopkinson, Hartle, Farrimond, Threlfall, Edwards, Rimmer, Holden, Stevens, Phythian, Hill, Pilkington
Scorers: Crawford 83, 88 / Holden 37. Ref: W Clements
Dour Bolton try to preserve their lead with tactics that upset Town fans. Roars of disapproval greet a bad foul by Syd Farrimond and this seems to galvanise Town. Crawford shoulder-charges keeper and ball over the line and then hooks a dramatic winner after Moran's shot was blocked.

23. A MANCHESTER C 23/12 — Att 18,376 — Pos 5 — Pt 27 (L) — F-A 0-3 — H-T 0-2
Town: Bailey, Carberry, Compton, Baxter, Nelson, Elsworthy, Stephenson, Moran, Crawford, Phillips, Leadbetter
Man C: Trautmann, Betts, Sear, Cheetham, Leivers, Kennedy, Young, Hannah, Dobing, Hayes, Wagstaffe
Scorers: Hayes 9, Dobing 13, Young 47. Ref: R Langdale
On a bone-hard pitch, Joe Hayes' shot slips inside the near post of Bailey. Defensive hesitation gives Peter Dobing the time and space to head a second from a corner. Seventeen-year-old Neil Young goes on a great run and fires home at the second attempt after his first shot hits Baxter.

24. H LEICESTER 26/12 — Att 18,146 — Pos 4 — Pt 29 (W) — F-A 1-0 — H-T 0-0
Town: Bailey, Carberry, Compton, Baxter, Nelson, Elsworthy, Stephenson, Moran, Crawford, Phillips, Owen
Leicester: Banks, Chalmers, Norman, McLintock, King, Keyworth, Riley, Walsh, Cheesebrough, Appleton, Mitten
Scorers: Crawford 67. Ref: A Holland
Leadbetter is out with a knee injury after 156 games in a row. His deputy Owen crosses for Crawford to despatch the winning goal. Carberry clears off the line from Jim Walsh. After his earlier heroics, hot-shot Phillips is going through a quiet spell - to the relief of Gordon Banks.

25. H WEST BROM 13/1 — Att 18,378 — Pos 3 — Pt 31 (W) — F-A 3-0 — H-T 1-0
Town: Bailey, Carberry, Compton, Baxter, Nelson, Elsworthy, Stephenson, Moran, Crawford, Phillips, Leadbetter
West Brom: Wallace, Howe, Williams, Robson, Jones, Drury, Jackson, Burnside, Smith, Kevan, Clarke
Scorers: Stephenson 16, Moran 50, Lead' 89. Ref: M Fussey
Stephenson steers a low drive past Jock Wallace. Moran is put clear by Stephenson's pass and smashes the ball home. The returning Leadbetter outshines the England international Bobby Robson and makes up for a missed sitter by cracking home a fierce angled drive in the final minute.

26. A BIRMINGHAM 20/1 — Att 26,968 — Pos 4 — Pt 31 (L) — F-A 1-3 — H-T 0-2
Town: Hall, Carberry, Compton, Baxter, Nelson, Elsworthy, Stephenson, Moran, Crawford, Phillips, Leadbetter
Birmingham: Schofield, Lynn, Sissons, Hennessey, Smith, Beard, Hellawell, Bloomfield, Harris, Leek, Auld
Scorers: Crawford 53 / Leek 10, 26, Baxter 50 (og). Ref: J Pickles
Hall steps in for tonsilitis victim Bailey and is beaten early by Ken Leek's breakaway goal. The appropriately-named Welshman cracks in a vicious shot on the turn. Crawford is gifted a goal by a John Schofield blunder. Baxter passes back, not realising Hall has strayed out of goal.

27. H EVERTON 3/2 — Att 22,572 — Pos 2 — Pt 33 (W) — F-A 4-2 — H-T 3-1
Town: Bailey, Carberry, Compton, Baxter, Nelson, Elsworthy, Stephenson, Moran, Crawford, Phillips, Leadbetter
Everton: Dunlop, Parker, Green, Gabriel, Labone, Harris, Bingham, Collins, Young, Vernon, Lill
Scorers: Phillips 6, Moran 35, Elsworthy 42, Crawford 58 / Bingham 24, Harris 89. Ref: H Horner
Billy Bingham forces in an equaliser after Phillips sidefooted Town ahead. Moran's glorious header is followed by Elsworthy heading in a free-kick. Lively Crawford deserves his goal, squeezed in from an 'impossible' angle after he started the move himself with a long run from deep.

28. A FULHAM 10/2 — Att 25,209 — Pos 3 — Pt 35 (W) — F-A 2-1 — H-T 1-1
Town: Bailey, Carberry, Compton, Baxter, Nelson, Elsworthy, Stephenson, Moran, Crawford, Phillips, Leadbetter
Fulham: Hewkins, Cohen, Mealand, Mullery, Dodgin, Lowe, Cook, Leggatt, Henderson, Haynes, Metchick
Scorers: Stephenson 26, Crawford 78 / Mullery 13. Ref: R Leafe
A ninth defeat on the trot for Bedford Jezzard's men, despite a bright start. Alan Mullery is the pick of the home side and cracks in a brilliantly-taken opener. Stephenson's cross is punched into his own net by stand-in Ken Hewkins. Stephenson's superb pass sets up Crawford's winner.

29. A WEST HAM 24/2 — Att 27,763 — Pos 3 — Pt 36 (D) — F-A 2-2 — H-T 1-1
Town: Bailey, Carberry, Compton, Baxter, Nelson, Elsworthy, Stephenson, Moran, Crawford, Phillips, Leadbetter
West Ham: Leslie, Kirkup, Bond, Bovington, Brown, Moore, Scott, Boyce, Sealey, Dick, Musgrove
Scorers: Leadbetter 20, Phillips 79p / Dick 7, Kirkup 46. Ref: P Brandwood
Ex-Hammer Nelson makes an error and John Dick fires in. Crawford hits the bar but Leadbetter is on hand to net. Baxter makes an acrobatic goal-line clearance. Joe Kirkup's long-range shot is helped into the net by Bailey. Kirkup handles and Phillips smashes home a penalty leveller.

30. H SHEFFIELD UTD 3/3 — Att 20,158 — Pos 2 — Pt 38 (W) — F-A 4-0 — H-T 2-0
Town: Bailey, Carberry, Compton, Baxter, Nelson, Elsworthy, Stephenson, Moran, Crawford, Phillips, Leadbetter
Sheffield Utd: Hopkinson, Coldwell, Shaw G, Richardson, Shaw J, Summers, Allchurch, Russell, Pace, Kettleborough, Hartle
Scorers: Moran 12, Leadbetter 25, Crawford 58, 75. Ref: E Jennings
A terrific shot by quick-thinking Moran sets Town on their way and Leadbetter bustles in a second goal. The slippery Crawford poaches two goals and his display will do his England World Cup selection hopes no harm. However, the poor form of partner Phillips remains a mystery.

31. H SHEFFIELD WED 9/3 — Att 23,713 — Pos 2 — Pt 40 (W) — F-A 2-1 — H-T 1-1
Town: Bailey, Carberry, Compton, Baxter, Nelson, Elsworthy, Stephenson, Moran, Crawford, Phillips, Leadbetter
Sheffield Wed: Springett, Johnson, Megson, Hardy, Swann, Kay, Wilkinson, Dobson, Young, Fantham, Finney
Scorers: Crawford 29, Stephenson 86 / Dobson 6. Ref: C Woan
Colin Dobson flicks a header past Bailey to give Vic Buckingham's men the lead. Crawford converts a low cross to level. A tremendous battle is decided late when Stephenson races on to Crawford's pass, sweeping between two defenders before netting. It's an 11th successive home win.

Ipswich Town — season match record (games 32–42, 1961–62)

#	H/A	Date	Opponent	Pos	Res	Score	Opp Pos	Pts	Attendance
32	A	14/3	TOTTENHAM	2	W	3-1	3	42	**51,098**
33	H	17/3	BLACKPOOL	2	D	1-1	9	43	22,450
34	A	24/3	NOTT'M FOREST	2	D	1-1	16	44	26,053
35	A	28/3	LEICESTER	2	W	2-0	16	46	19,068
36	H	31/3	WOLVERHAMPTON	1	W	3-2	15	48	23,153
37	A	7/4	MANCHESTER U	2	L	0-5	14	48	24,976
38	H	14/4	CARDIFF	1	W	1-0	21	50	17,693
39	H	20/4	ARSENAL	2	D	2-2	7	51	**30,649**
40	A	21/4	CHELSEA	1	D	2-2	22	52	28,462
41	A	23/4	ARSENAL	1	W	3-0	9	54	44,694
42	H	28/4	ASTON VILLA	1	W	2-0	8	56	28,932

Attendance — Home Average 22,815 / Away 26,339

---

32. TOTTENHAM (A) — W 3-1
Ipswich: Bailey, Carberry, Compton, Baxter, Nelson, Elsworthy, Stephenson, Moran, Crawford, Phillips, Leadbetter
Tottenham: Brown, Baker, Henry, Blanchflower, Norman, Marchi, Jones, White, Smith, Greaves, Medwin
Crawford 8, Phillips 41, 71 / Greaves 9. Ref: W Haynes
Crawford tricks his way through for a fine goal, but Jimmy Greaves matches it by making a monkey of Bailey seconds later. Phillips ends the debate over his form with an inspired display. He heads Town ahead after Stephenson hits a post. His well-placed shot clinches a fabulous win.

33. BLACKPOOL (H) — D 1-1
Ipswich: Bailey, Carberry, Compton, Baxter, Nelson, Elsworthy, Stephenson, Moran, Crawford, Phillips, Leadbetter
Blackpool: Harvey, Armfield, Martin, Crawford, Gratrix, Durie, Hill, Hauser, Charnley, Parry, Horne
Moran 14 / Charnley 90. Ref: G McCabe
Crawford goes on a dazzling run to create a goal for Moran. Phillips breaks his thumb in a collision with Bryan Harvey, a stand-in for Tony Waiters. Town are not at their best and Ronnie Suart's men deserve an equaliser 12 seconds from time as Ray Charnley despatches a rebound.

34. NOTT'M FOREST (A) — D 1-1
Ipswich: Bailey, Carberry, Compton, Baxter, Nelson, Elsworthy, Stephenson, Moran, Crawford, Curtis, Leadbetter
Forest: Grummitt, Wiland, Gray, Winfield, McKinlay, Iley, Rowland, Vowden, Julians, Quigley, Le Flem
Moran 18 / Julians 45. Ref: R Smith
Bailey is busy and his saves keep Town in the game. Moran surprises Andy Beattie's side by beating Peter Grummitt at the second attempt. John Rowland goes round Compton to set up Len Julians. Crawford looks tired after England duty and Leadbetter plays with a stomach upset.

35. LEICESTER (A) — W 2-0
Ipswich: Bailey, Carberry, Compton, Pickett, Nelson, Elsworthy, Stephenson, Moran, Crawford, Curtis, Leadbetter
Leicester: Banks, Chalmers, Norman, McLintock, King, Appleton, Riley, Walsh, Cheesebrough, Keyworth, Stringfellow
Crawford 8, Stephenson 48. Ref: K Collinge
Moran's cross is headed smartly home by inrushing Crawford. Stephenson steers the ball in through a crowded box against his former team. Matt Gillies' side miss several chances. Town go level on points with Burnley at the top and the impossible dream takes a step nearer reality.

36. WOLVERHAMPTON (H) — W 3-2
Ipswich: Bailey, Carberry, Compton, Pickett, Nelson, Elsworthy, Stephenson, Moran, Crawford, Phillips, Leadbetter
Wolves: Finlayson, Stuart, Showell, Kirkham, Slater, Flowers, Crowe, Murray, McParland, Broadbent, Murray
Phillips 20p, Crawford 32, Moran 88 / Flowers 24, McParland 59. Ref: S Yates
Crawford is hauled down for a penalty, but Ron Flowers is quick to equalise with a 25-yard piledriver. New signing Peter McParland levels Crawford's 32nd of the season. Moran's winner at the death brings the house down. Ipswich lead the nation for the first time in club history.

37. MANCHESTER U (A) — L 0-5
Ipswich: Bailey, Carberry, Compton, Baxter, Nelson, Elsworthy, Stephenson, Moran, Curtis, Phillips, Leadbetter
Man U: Briggs, Brennan, Dunne, Stiles, Faulkes, Setters, Muir, Giles, Quixall, Charlton, McMillan
Quixall 14, 20, 50, Stiles 84, [Setters 85]. Ref: R Simons
Albert Quixall notches a fine hat-trick and is badly fouled by Nelson for his trouble. Town are resigned to a first League defeat since January long before the end. Bobby Charlton strikes wood three times. Half-backs Nobby Stiles and Maurice Setters exploit vast open spaces late on.

38. CARDIFF (H) — W 1-0
Ipswich: Bailey, Carberry, Compton, Baxter, Nelson, Pickett, Stephenson, Moran, Crawford, Phillips, Leadbetter
Cardiff: John, Stitfall, Milne, Baker, Rankmore, Hole, McCarthy, King, Charles, Durban, Pickrell
Moran 24. Ref: J Loynton
After the Old Trafford nightmare, Town look very tentative but ride their luck when Barry Hole hits the crossbar. From a Stephenson cross, Crawford heads goalwards and Moran helps it over the line. Town hang on grimly and defeat for Burnley means the leadership is regained.

39. ARSENAL (H) — D 2-2
Ipswich: Bailey, Carberry, Compton, Baxter, Nelson, Elsworthy, Stephenson, Moran, Crawford, Phillips, Leadbetter
Arsenal: Kelsey, McGill, McCullough, Brown, Neill, Petts, McLeod, Griffiths, Strong, Eastham, Skirton
Phillips 64p, Leadbetter 85 / McLeod 55, Eastham 59. Ref: G Grundy
A record crowd sees a tense struggle. A double blow as John McLeod drives beyond Bailey's reach and George Eastham nets a remarkable overhead kick. Phillips converts after Crawford is hauled down and then it's all Ipswich. Pandemonium as Leadbetter scrambles a late leveller.

40. CHELSEA (A) — D 2-2
Ipswich: Bailey, Carberry, Compton, Baxter, Nelson, Elsworthy, Stephenson, Moran, Crawford, Phillips, Leadbetter
Chelsea: McNally, Shellito, Butler, Malcolm, Mortimore, Upton, Brabrook, Murray, Bridges, Blunstone, Harrison
Crawford 63, Phillips 77p / Brabrook 26, Bridges 37. Ref: L Hamer
It's neck and neck with Burnley at the top, but both title rivals are dropping points. Peter Brabrook nets a deflected shot and Barry Bridges heads past Bailey. Town rally after the break and win a precious and rather lucky point via the spot after John Mortimore inexplicably handles.

41. ARSENAL (A) — W 3-0
Ipswich: Bailey, Carberry, Compton, Baxter, Nelson, Elsworthy, Stephenson, Moran, Crawford, Phillips, Leadbetter
Arsenal: Kelsey, McGill, McCullough, Clamp, Neill, Petts, McLeod, Griffiths, Strong, Eastham, Clapton
Phillips 14, Crawford 18, 80. Ref: A Holland
Phillips nets a fine header from Stephenson's corner. Crawford beats Kelsey emphatically after a Phillips dummy. Crawford stuns Highbury, beating two men before nutmegging Terry Neill and firing home. This top-rate display puts the title within grasp as Burnley continue to stutter.

42. ASTON VILLA (H) — W 2-0
Ipswich: Bailey, Carberry, Compton, Baxter, Nelson, Elsworthy, Stephenson, Moran, Crawford, Phillips, Leadbetter
Villa: Sims, Lee, Aitken, Crowe, Sleeuwenhoek, Deakin, McEwan, Baker, Thomson, Dougan, Ewing
Crawford 72, 76. Ref: E Crawford
Joe Mercer's Villa fight hard and nervy Town rarely threaten for over 70 minutes. Then Elsworthy hits the bar and Crawford dives to net the rebound. Sheer persistence gets him another. Burnley can only draw with Chelsea and the title is won! Ecstatic supporters rush on to celebrate.

LEAGUE DIVISION 1 (CUP-TIES) SEASON 1961-62

Manager: Alf Ramsey

League Cup

			F-A	H-T	Scorers, Times, and Referees	1	2	3	4	5	6	7	8	9	10	11
1 H 11/9	MANCHESTER C	5 W 14,919 11	4-2	3-0	Moran 29, 35, Crawford 44, 64, Betts 48p, Compton 54 (og) Ref: P Bye	Hall *Trautmann*	Carberry *Betts*	Compton *Sear*	Baxter *Cheetham*	Nelson *Ewing*	Elsworthy *Kennedy*	Stephenson *Barlow*	Moran *Dobing*	Crawford *Hannah*	Phillips *Hayes*	Leadbetter *Wagstaffe*
2 A 3/10	SWANSEA	6 D 13,541 2:15	3-3	0-3	Phillips 53, Steph' 65, Crawford 87 / Comp'2 (og), Nel'10 (og), Davies R 24 Ref: R Leafe	Hall *Dwyer*	Milward *Saunders*	Compton *Griffiths*	Baxter *Johnson*	Nelson *Nurse*	Elsworthy *Davies P*	Stephenson *Jones*	Moran *Davies R*	Crawford *Dodson*	Phillips *Williams H*	Leadbetter *Williams G*
2R H 24/10	SWANSEA	4 W 11,010 2:15	3-2	2-2	Phillips 38p, Moran 44, Steph' 65 / Hughes 14, Reynolds 26 Ref: R Leafe	Bailey *Dwyer*	Carberry *Saunders*	Compton *Griffiths*	Baxter *Johnson*	Nelson *Nurse*	Elsworthy *Hughes*	Stephenson *Jones*	Moran *Morgans*	Crawford *Dodson*	Phillips *Reynolds*	Leadbetter *Webster*
3 A 21/11	ASTON VILLA	4 W 22,000 16	3-2	2-0	Leadbetter 15, Phillips 35, 77p / Burrows 47, 75p Ref: R Tinkler	Bailey *Sims*	Carberry *Lee*	Compton *Aitken*	Baxter *Crowe*	Nelson *Sleeuwenhoek*	Elsworthy *Deakin*	Owen *McParland*	Moran *Wylie*	Curtis *Thomson*	Phillips *O'Neill*	Leadbetter *Burrows*
4 A 11/12	BLACKBURN	3 L 11,071 17	1-4	1-1	Phillips 40p / Lawther 23, Byrom 68, (Pickering 75p, 81) Ref: V James	Bailey *Else*	Carberry *Taylor*	Compton *Newton*	Baxter *Clayton*	Nelson *Woods*	Elsworthy *McGrath*	Stephenson *Lawther*	Moran *Byrom*	Crawford *Pickering*	Phillips *Douglas*	Leadbetter *Ratcliffe*

Moran slots in a through ball and then waltzes round Bert Trautmann. Crawford piles on City's agony with an angled drive. Barrie Betts tucks in a penalty after Baxter impedes Joe Hayes and then Compton deflects in Roy Cheetham's header. Crawford bursts through to kill City off.

Compton's back-pass slides past horrified Hall and then Nelson heads a Reg Davies lob into his own net. The nightmare continues as a Davies cross swirls straight in. Phillips rounds Mel Nurse to net and then Stephenson fires in a cracker. Moran's late cross is hooked in by Crawford.

Trevor Morris' side get another great start. Brian Hughes scrambles in a corner and Brayley Reynolds converts Colin Webster's pass. Moran is brought down for a penalty and then Moran equalises after Phillips' effort is parried. Stephenson beats Nurse and cuts in to shoot a late winner.

Leadbetter darts in to score and Phillips converts a comfortable header. Harry Burrows shoots under Bailey and later equalises after a Nelson handball. Villa look the better side but fall behind when Charlie Aitken handles in the area. Town miss Crawford, away on international duty.

Jack Marshall's young side pepper the Town goal with shots. Phillips cancels out Ian Lawther's opener with his 23rd of the season in just 24 games. After 17-year-old John Byrom hits the target, Rovers don't look back. Fred Pickering's pair includes a penalty after Carberry handled.

FA Cup

			F-A	H-T	Scorers, Times, and Referees	1	2	3	4	5	6	7	8	9	10	11
3 H 6/1	LUTON	4 D 18,450 2:11	1-1	1-0	Phillips 1 / Chandler 57 Ref: K Dagnall	Bailey *Baynham*	Carberry *McNally*	Compton *Bramwell*	Baxter *Morton*	Nelson *Cope*	Elsworthy *Pacey*	Stephenson *Walden*	Moran *Ashworth*	Crawford *Chandler*	Phillips *McKechnie*	Owen *Legate*
3R A 10/1	LUTON	4 D 23,818 2:11 aet	1-1	1-0	Elsworthy 16 / Pacey 76 Ref: K Dagnall	Bailey *Baynham*	Carberry *McNally*	Compton *Bramwell*	Baxter *Morton*	Nelson *Cope*	Elsworthy *Pacey*	Stephenson *Walden*	Moran *Ashworth*	Crawford *Chandler*	Phillips *McKechnie*	Owen *Legate*
3RR N 15/1 (at Highbury)	LUTON	3 W 29,438 2:10	5-1	3-0	Moran 2, Phillips 6, 16p, Steph' 79, 86 / Ashworth 56 Ref: R Mann	Hall *Baynham*	Carberry *McNally*	Compton *Bramwell*	Baxter *Morton*	Nelson *Kelly*	Elsworthy *Pacey*	Stephenson *Walden*	Moran *Ashworth*	Crawford *Chandler*	Phillips *McKechnie*	Leadbetter *Legate*
4 A 27/1	NORWICH	4 D 39,890 2:12	1-1	0-0	Leadbetter 53 / Allcock 48 Ref: K Aston	Bailey *Kennon*	Carberry *Thurlow*	Compton *Ashman*	Baxter *McCrohan*	Nelson *Butler*	Elsworthy *Mullett*	Stephenson *Mannion*	Moran *Allcock*	Crawford *Conway*	Phillips *Hill*	Leadbetter *Lythgoe*
4R H 30/1	NORWICH	4 L 29,798 2:12	1-2	0-1	Crawford 49 / Allcock 40, 88 Ref: K Aston	Bailey *Kennon*	Carberry *Thurlow*	Compton *Ashman*	Baxter *McCrohan*	Nelson *Butler*	Elsworthy *Mullett*	Stephenson *Mannion*	Moran *Allcock*	Crawford *Conway*	Phillips *Hill*	Leadbetter *Lythgoe*

Phillips heads in a Stephenson cross in the first minute, but on a slushy pitch Town fail to impress after this bright start. Robin Chandler scores what will be the only senior goal of his career after he is set up by Alec Ashworth. Luton are denied a penalty when Ashworth is hauled down.

Elsworthy sends a 20-yard thunderbolt past Ron Baynham following a corner. Fouls by Compton, Nelson and Elsworthy anger home fans who jeer Town off at the interval. Tom McKechnie feeds Dave Pacey, who crashes home off the underside of the bar. Deadlock after 210 minutes.

Highbury stages the next instalment. A major blunder by skipper Bob Morton as he chooses to kick against a howling gale. The conditions undoubtedly help Town get off to a dream start. Luton inevitably improve after the break, but it is far too late and Stephenson wraps things up.

Fans unable to make the trip watch on closed circuit TV at Ipswich's Baths Hall. Terry Allcock heads in a Derek Lythgoe cross, but Leadbetter steers a neat response past Sandy Kennon minutes later. Local derby tension stifles the match. Phillips again looks mysteriously out of touch.

Terry Allcock volleys the Canaries ahead, but Crawford hooks in a corner after the break. Town have 75 per cent of the play and force 12 corners to City's one, but the visitors have the last laugh. Lethal Allcock swoops to convert a Gerry Mannion cross with extra-time looming.

Home / Away

	P	W	D	L	F	A	W	D	L	F	A	Pts
1 IPSWICH	42	17	2	2	58	28	7	6	8	35	39	56
2 Burnley	42	14	4	3	57	26	7	7	7	44	41	53
3 Tottenham	42	14	4	3	59	34	7	6	8	29	35	52
4 Everton	42	17	2	2	64	21	3	9	9	24	33	51
5 Sheffield Utd	42	13	5	3	37	23	6	4	11	24	46	47
6 Sheffield Wed	42	14	4	3	47	23	6	2	13	25	35	46
7 Aston Villa	42	13	5	3	45	20	5	3	13	20	36	44
8 West Ham	42	11	6	4	49	37	6	4	11	27	45	44
9 West Brom	42	10	7	4	50	23	6	6	10	33	44	43
10 Arsenal	42	9	6	6	39	31	7	5	9	32	41	43
11 Bolton	42	11	7	3	35	22	5	3	13	27	44	42
12 Manchester C	42	11	3	7	46	38	6	4	11	32	43	41
13 Blackpool	42	10	4	7	41	30	5	7	9	29	45	41
14 Leicester	42	12	2	7	38	27	5	4	12	34	44	40
15 Manchester U	42	10	3	8	44	31	5	6	10	28	44	39
16 Blackburn	42	10	6	5	33	22	4	5	12	17	36	39
17 Birmingham	42	9	6	6	37	35	5	4	12	28	46	38
18 Wolves	42	8	7	6	38	34	5	3	13	35	52	36
19 Nott'm Forest	42	12	4	5	39	23	1	6	14	24	56	36
20 Fulham	42	8	3	10	38	34	5	4	12	28	40	33
21 Cardiff	42	6	9	6	30	33	3	5	13	20	48	32
22 Chelsea	42	7	7	7	34	29	2	3	16	29	65	28
	924	246	106	110	958	624	110	106	246	624	958	924

Odds & ends

Double wins: (5) WBA, Cardiff, Sheffield W, Tottenham, Leicester.
Double losses: (1) Manchester C.

Won from behind: (5) Tottenham (h), Bolton (h), Fulham (a), Sheffield W (h), Swansea (h, LC).
Lost from in front: (1) Fulham (h).

High spots: Winning the title – one of the least expected achievements in Football League history.
Another productive season for the Crawford-Phillips partnership.
Doing the 'double' over reigning champions Tottenham.
Two classic goal-filled encounters with title-rivals Burnley.
A superb win at mighty Arsenal to set up the final week's drama.
The lack of injuries that enabled Ramsey to employ a settled side.

Low spots: The last-gasp home defeat by Norwich in the FA Cup.
Ted Phillips' mysterious spell of poor form after Christmas.
The hammering at Old Trafford, which nearly derailed the title chase.

Hat-tricks: (1) Ray Crawford v Chelsea (h).
Opposing hat-tricks: (2) Derek Temple (Everton), Albert Quixall (Man U).
Ever-presents: (2) D Moran, A Nelson (L Carberry – League only).
Leading scorer: (37) Ray Crawford.

Appearances / Goals

	Appearances			Goals			
	Lge	LC	FAC	Lge	LC	FAC	Tot
Bailey, Roy	37	3	4				
Baxter, Billy	40	5	5				
Carberry, Larry	42	4	5				
Crawford, Ray	41	4	5	33	3	1	37
Compton, John	39	5	5				
Curtis, Dermot	4	1					
Elsworthy, John	41	5	5	2		1	3
Hall, Wilf	5	2	1				
Leadbetter, Jimmy	41	5	3	8	1	1	10
Malcolm, Ken	3						
Millward, Doug		1					
Moran, Doug	42	5	5	14	3	1	18
Nelson, Andy	42	5	5				
Owen, Aled	1	1	2				
Phillips, Ted	40	5	5	28	5	3	36
Pickett, Reg	3						
Stephenson, Roy	41	4	5	7	2	2	11
(own-goals)				1			1
17 players used	462	55	55	93	14	9	116

LIST OF SUBSCRIBERS

VOTES FOR THE MOST IMPORTANT IPSWICH TOWN PLAYER 1961-62

Subscriber	Vote
Michael Allen	Ray Crawford
Chris Austin	Ray Crawford
Peter Baker	Ray Crawford
Veronica Barley	Ray Crawford
Gerry Barrack	Ray Crawford
Una Bauly	Roy Stephenson
Brian Stephen Bell	Billy Baxter
Alan Benedick	Jimmy Leadbetter
Joseph Berry	Ray Crawford
Pat Boon	Ray Crawford
Mr John Booth	Ray Crawford
Nigel Boreham	Ray Crawford
DJ Bullock	Jimmy Leadbetter
Mr BFJ Catchpole	Ted Phillips
Charles R Clarke	Ray Crawford
David Clarke	Ray Crawford
John Clarke	Ray Crawford
Mr W S Clements	Ray Crawford
Roy Clements	
Mr G Cocksedge	Ray Crawford
Graham Cole	Billy Baxter
M J Cook	Ray Crawford
Mr R Cooper	Ray Crawford
John Cross	Ray Crawford
Ian Crowe	Jimmy Leadbetter
David Cull	Doug Millward
David Emsden	Ray Crawford
Sidney H Gardner	John Elsworthy
Andrew Griffiths	Jimmy Leadbetter
Brian M Grimwood	Ray Crawford
PC Hadgraft	Dennis Thrower
Paul Hadgraft	Ted Phillips
Miss C Hale	Ray Crawford
Colin Handley	Ray Crawford
Gary Hannam	Mick Mills
Arild Sorknes Hansen	Ray Crawford
Gill & John Hardy	Ray Crawford
Paul Hart	Ted Phillips
Karl Harvey	Doug Moran
Carl Hastings	Billy Baxter
Paul Hedger	Ray Crawford
Gerald E Hogg	Ray Crawford
Garry Hudson	Ray Crawford
Michael Hugman	Ray Crawford
Mark Jackson	Ray Crawford
Roger Jarrold	Ted Phillips
Dave Johnson	Ray Crawford
Trevor Johnson	Ray Crawford
Paul Keeble	Ray Crawford
Percy Kent	Ray Crawford
Bill Knights	Ray Crawford
John Kolodziej	Ray Crawford
Michael Lambton	John Elsworthy
Derek Lay	Ray Crawford
Ian & Averil Lockwood	Ray Crawford
Fred Maddison	Billy Baxter
Carl & Alison Mann	Ray Crawford
William Martin	Ray Crawford
John May	Ray Crawford
Brian Mills	Ray Crawford
Mr KD Newman	Ray Crawford
Nigel Richard Nunn	'entire squad'
Michael Oakley	Ray Crawford
Benny Osborne	Jimmy Leadbetter
Alan Peck	Ray Crawford
Robert Porter	Ted Phillips
Ben Ramsey	Ray Crawford
Paul Ramsey	Ray Crawford
Wayne Rice	Jimmy Leadbetter
George Ridley	John Elsworthy
Paul D Rose	Ted Phillips
Wilf Ruffles	Ray Crawford
Keith A Savage	Ray Crawford
Richard Simnett	John Elsworthy
Norman Skedge	Ray Crawford
Duncan Skippings	Ray Crawford
Andrew Slugocki	Ray Crawford
Martin CF Smith	Jimmy Leadbetter
Trevor Smith	Jimmy Leadbetter
Richard Stocken	
Martin Talbot	Ted Phillips
Jane Tew	Ray Crawford
Richard Townsend	Jimmy Leadbetter
Julie Tunney	Ray Crawford
Andrew Vinyard	Ted Phillips
Ben Vulliamy	Ray Crawford
Daniel Vulliamy	Ted Phillips
Russell Walker	Ted Phillips
Brian Whatling	Ray Crawford
Nicholas Wilkes	Ray Crawford
SG Wise	Matt Holland

MOST IMPORTANT IPSWICH PLAYERS 1961-62

1st	Ray Crawford
2nd	Ted Phillips
3rd	Jimmy Leadbetter